# COUNTDOWN

## A NEWSMAN LOOKS AT THE RAPTURE

DAN BETZER

Gospel Publishing House/Springfield, Mo. 65802

02-0481

*COUNTDOWN*



*Library of Congress Catalog Card Number 79-53943*
*International Standard Book Number 0-88243-481-0*
*Printed in the United States of America*

# INTRODUCTION

I have not always been in the ministry. For nearly 10 years, I pounded the beat as a news reporter for radio and television. It has been said that newscasting is rather like a narcotic—it is very difficult to get out of your system. That's probably a correct assessment. Even today I enjoy visiting newsrooms and watching reporters in action.

Different worlds were open to me in my role as a newscaster. I was privileged to interview many of the world's famous and infamous in their most public hours—John Glenn after his historic space shot; state governors shortly after their elections (or defeats); nationally known sports figures; convicted murderers on their way to death row; outstanding businessmen and educators; even a president of the United States.

A newscaster observes disaster and heartbreak firsthand. I have seen highway accidents that have claimed multiple lives. I have seen corpses stacked like cordwood in a shack following a killing spree; flood victims weeping silently by their destroyed homes; politicians broken on the wheel of public opinion. And I have seen men and women entering the courtroom on trial for their lives.

Year after year a newsman watches the play unfold before him. It's a constant parade of humanity: beauty queens, thugs, connivers, opinion-makers, the high society crowd, ball players, movie stars, union enforcers, princes of the religious world—on and on they go.

Newspeople, like law enforcement personnel, grow cynical rather quickly. The old saw, "Good news doesn't sell," is correct. The horror stories of mankind get the attention. So that's where the good reporter does his digging.

In rare idle moments in the newsroom, I enjoyed sitting back with a cup of coffee, letting my mind wander over a favorite theme: What would it be like to be on duty on the night (or day) Christ returned for the Church? Where would the story break first—on the AP or UPI wire? on the local police scanner? a frantic citizen calling to inquire about missing friends? the disappearance of personnel from the radio staff?

A good newsstory should answer basic questions—who? why? what? where? when? how? What a demand it will be on a newscaster's professionalism to cover adequately the story of Christ's return! There is little doubt in my mind that he will have to wade through unbelievable panic to get his story.

Recently, a giant DC-10 crashed on takeoff in Chicago, claiming 275 lives. Every television show was interrupted for the story. Late shows were delayed so the networks could give additional coverage to the tragedy.

Consider what it will be like when millions upon

millions of people suddenly vanish! Reporters used to describe a big story: "That's the biggest story since the Second Coming . . . ."

I have no doubt that radio and TV shows will be preempted for days; that print media will carry little else for issue after issue. The event so few give any thought to now will be the only event they will think of one of these days.

When I entered the news field, I knew little about prophetic Scripture. That was not very wise on my part, since fully a third of the Word of God was prophetic at the time of its writing. A careful perusal of these sacred Scriptures is of great benefit to the believer.

During my news years, as I saw incredible things happening around the world, my attention became riveted on prophecy. I began to study Daniel, Ezekiel, the Book of Revelation, parts of the Psalms, and other Scripture passages given to prophetic themes.

Tucked into the excitement of my study was a trip I made several years ago. I flew to Athens and took a taxi to Piraeus where I caught passage on a Greek freighter. Within several days the old ship brought me to the breathtakingly beautiful harbor of an island in the Aegean Sea. I disembarked and began making my way through the little whitewashed town. Someone who spoke English told me where I could rent a horse. All I could find at the stable was a rather small donkey. The keeper told me the little beast could surely carry me across the mountain. Dubious, I paid the rental fee, climbed aboard the protesting animal's back, and began my quest.

I was on the Isle of Patmos, a double mountain

that rises from the blue waters of the Aegean. When the sun hits it just right, it is indescribably lovely. In the apostle John's day, it was a Roman concentration camp. John, the only one of the original 12 apostles to escape violent death, had been banished to Patmos for his faith in Jesus Christ.

Within several hours, my "faithful steed" had borne me to the top of the first mountain, upon which stands a huge monastery. I asked one of the fathers where I might find the Cave of St. John. He gave me good directions and, within minutes, I had found it. There, according to tradition, John received the vision of the end times.

In a most difficult place, under the bleakest of circumstances, John found himself in the Spirit on the Lord's Day. It is worth noting that such a divine revelation was received in a prison cave, not in a vaulted cathedral. Perhaps other prisoners that day cursed their lives, finding nothing on Patmos but loneliness and hurt. But John was in the presence of God.

The others heard the soldiers' coarse voices. John heard the angels and the singing of the redeemed saints of the ages, whose song echoed as the voice of many waters and as the voice of a great thunder. The others saw only rocks. John saw lamps of fire burning before the Throne. He saw a sea of crystal, and six-winged beasts flying overhead saying, "Holy, holy, holy."

John beheld angels numbering 10,000 times 10,000—a great multitude—saying, "Worthy is the Lamb!" While he watched, every creature in heaven and on earth and under the sea cried, "Blessing, and honor, and glory, and power, be unto him that sitteth upon the throne, and unto the Lamb for ever and ever" (Revelation 5:13).

John sat where no other man had been, while those about him blasphemed the Creator, unaware that eternity had touched the island of death.

During my years as a newscaster, I saw things that an unregenerated newsman never would have seen. It was not just an unending march of disjointed stories that paraded before me. Each day was a fresh revelation that God was in full control of the world and that Jesus' coming was the surest thing on earth.

I felt a small affinity with John on Patmos. While I saw death and killing and human suffering, I saw a master plan unfolding. It made me a staunch believer that the Bible is literally true. And I proclaim that conviction without the slightest hesitation.

This book tells of the return of our lovely Lord as seen through the eyes of an old "retired" newsman. It begins with a simulated night in the newsroom on the day Jesus returns for His church. Other parts of the book tell of the bits and pieces of our lives today that may look like a puzzle—but, when put together, form a magnificently beautiful picture. It is a picture of Jesus coming in clouds of glory to take us home.

Even now the words of the great old camp meeting song "Oh, I Want to See Him" flood my soul:

*As I journey thro' the land singing as I go,*
*Pointing souls to Calvary—to the crimson flow,*

*Many arrows pierce my soul from without, within;*
*But my Lord leads me on, thro' Him I must win.*

*O, I want to see Him, look upon His face,*
*There to sing forever of His saving grace;*
*On the streets of glory let me lift my voice;*
*Cares all past, home at last, ever to rejoice.*

# CONTENTS


1 The Night Christ Returns . . . . . . . . . . . . . . . . 11

2 Signs . . . . . . . . . . . . . . . . . . . . . . . . . . . . . . 37

3 The Disappearance . . . . . . . . . . . . . . . . . . . 43

4 Diadems and Ashes . . . . . . . . . . . . . . . . . . . . 50

5 Meanwhile, Back on Earth . . . . . . . . . . . . . . 68

6 The Tribulation . . . . . . . . . . . . . . . . . . . . . . 77

7 Armageddon . . . . . . . . . . . . . . . . . . . . . . . . . 89

8 The Judgment of Sinners . . . . . . . . . . . . . . . . 98

9 What Will It Be Like In Heaven? . . . . . . . 106

# 1

# THE NIGHT CHRIST RETURNS

*(A fictitious account of a newsman on the night of the Rapture.)*

The sun was setting as Mike Mason wheeled his 3-year-old Buick into the TV station parking lot. The overhead mercury lights illuminated the west side of the stucco building as well as the 50 or so employee parking spaces.

This time of the evening was the toughest part of his work as a news anchorman. Rather than enjoying dinner at home with his wife Virginia, he carried a bag of burgers from a nearby drive-in. While other couples were preparing for an enjoyable evening with friends, Virginia was home alone—and he was preparing for another of the endless newscasts that seemed to glut his life.

Mike began his workday at WLIC-TV, Channel 2, each afternoon at 4. News director Josh Taggart handed him the list of the day's outstanding stories and Mike banged away at a vintage electric typewriter, preparing each segment in his own wording. It usually took several hours. The 29-minute newscast seldom contained more than 11 minutes of news. It also carried about 10 minutes of commercial time (each 30-second spot costing $300; making the 6 p.m. and 10 p.m. newscasts worth nearly $12,000 nightly), 4 minutes of weather reporting, and 5 minutes of sports.

Mason considered newscasts the simplest form of reporting there was because of their lack of depth. However, he never told anyone his thoughts. He was paid $22,500 yearly with assorted bonuses. And he never had to get his hands dirty. TV newscasting was an arm of show business as far as he was concerned. It always amused him to see Josh Taggart dashing around the newsroom, shouting out directives, trying to maintain a journalistic demeanor. He had so little to work with.

For example, Larry Conners had been assigned the weather reporting for nearly a year. Conners was not a meteorologist, but he didn't have to be. Channel 2 subscribed to the Accu-Weather service from State College, Pennsylvania. It was an adequate company that forecast showers and snow as well as the local weather bureau.

Conners had one major problem: he was a drunk. Early in his career he had been considered a possibility for movie stardom. Always a darkly handsome man, he kept himself in trim form by jogging 6 miles a day. Unfortunately, at the end of those miles there was usually a bar—and a willing barfly. When he began showing up late for shooting schedules, muffing the simplest of lines, and leaving a wake of fights and unpaid bills behind him, it was too much even for Paramount Studios. Conners had been given his walking papers.

He had tried various show business jobs—always with the same results. He was on the way down fast. The weather job at Channel 2 would be his last stop before making the list at the welfare bureau. Many nights, viewers wondered if there was something wrong with the audio of their TV sets when Conners' words were slurred and unintelligible.

Sports reporter Johnny Delbert was something else again. He was a full-blooded, dyed-in-the-wool "jock." An assassination story from Washington was never as important to Delbert as the ball scores. He never let anyone forget that he had been a 4-year All-Pro defensive safety for the Cleveland Browns. In 1964, Coach Blanton Collier had awarded him the game ball of the NFL Championship contest between the Browns and Baltimore. A sports magazine had given him a Corvette for being the game's Most Valuable Player.

His playing career had faded in the late 60's and he had landed the position of sports director at Channel 2. Delbert hung onto the job for dear life, making each day miserable for whomever happened to be his assistant. It was hard to remember their names; they never lasted more than a few months.

Mike Mason thought Johnny Delbert was the most obnoxious man he had ever met. But when the TV cameras were on, viewers considered the pair the best of friends. Their well-rehearsed ad-libs were often amusing—and almost always forced!

Co-anchorperson was Sally Tamm, by far the most qualified member of the news team. She had majored in journalism at Drake University in

Iowa. Tall and attractive, when properly made-up for the ruthless cameras, she approached each newscast with professionalism. The front office boys considered her a shoo-in for network employment soon. She and Mason formed an entertaining duo at 6 and 10 each evening, making the most devastating disaster stories seem enjoyable.

Mason entered the back door of the studio, walking through the control room on his way to the newsroom. The rest of the staff had not returned from dinner. He was the only member on duty. The others would show up about 7:30, but that was okay. He enjoyed eating alone and reading.

The 30-foot square newsroom was crowded with green metal desks, contrasting sharply with the yellow and black mottled carpet. Nineteen people were employed by Channel 2 news, including four full-time photographers. On the north wall, walnut shelves held three color monitors, a 3/4-inch video cassette deck, and a duplicator.

The other three walls were covered by various plaques and awards—some well-earned, others given perfunctorily by the NAB and the AP wire service. The news wire machine clicked incessantly behind a muffled closet door. The only other adornment in the drab room was a series of plants hung at various intervals. The building was kept spotless by the maintenance crew, a reflection of the boss' cleanliness fetish.

Channel 2 was one of the three television stations in the city, and it was rated number one. Mason could never quite decide if it was because they did such a crack job or because they had little or no competition. Channel 9 newscasts were anchored by Harry Foster, a man who believed he was meant for much higher things than TV—and it showed in his face. The third station was a UHF station, Channel 34, which was a farce.

Mason lit up a cigarette, finished his Coke, and picked up a trade magazine. He wanted to relax, if possible, before the hassle of putting together the 10 o'clock news.

But it was getting more and more difficult to relax these days. His wife Virginia was on a kick he couldn't understand at all. Two months ago the Masons had received an invitation to a Bible study to be held at a neighbor's home. They felt obligated to attend, and found a half-dozen couples present. The study was conducted by Pastor John Hennings of Calvary Assembly of God, a church Mike had never heard of. The preacher was a rotund, happy-faced man. He seemed to talk too loudly, Mike thought—or maybe it was his imagination. His speech concerned the first chapter of the Gospel of John. Mike didn't understand it at all—all that talk about darkness and light and Word made flesh. But Virginia enjoyed it thoroughly. As they walked home she made it clear she wanted to continue.

"Oh, Mike, it was so wonderful! I've never heard anything so refreshing. It's as if we can have a brand-new beginning to life. Let's go back next Saturday night."

Mike looked at his wife. She was beautiful. Virginia had always been the object of his deepest pride. "Darling, I didn't understand a word the man said. It's a lot of gobbledy-gook. Probably some new cult beginning. I'm not interested. You go alone if you want."

And Virginia did. A month later she told her husband the strangest thing he had ever heard. "Mike, I was saved tonight."

"You were what?"

"Saved. I accepted Jesus Christ as my Saviour. I'm a Christian now." Mike exploded, "Well, what do you think I am? A Swahili? I'm a Christian too. What's all this 'saved' jazz?"

"Sweetheart, Jesus told Nicodemus in the third chapter of John that he had to be born again. And Nicodemus was a good man, a religious person. But Jesus told him that his goodness wasn't enough. He needed a spiritual awakening. And I have found it, too. Mike, can you understand what I'm saying?"

The newsman touched his wife's hand gently. "Virginia, I don't understand. I'm sorry. But if it brings enjoyment to you, well—fine. But don't bug me with it. I'm not interested. Okay?"

"Sure, Mike. But this thing is real, and I want to share it with you. I won't bug you. But I will pray for you."

Mike laughed it off. "Yeah. You do that."

It was almost 8 p.m. Mike lit another cigarette and cleared his desk off to begin work. The truth of the matter was that Virginia was bugging him—even if she didn't mean to. She attended church twice on Sunday and even went to some Wednesday night prayer meetings, whatever they were. Plus the blasted Bible study on Saturday nights. She had quit smoking, which Mike didn't mind. But that was the only positive thing about the whole deal. Last week she had come up with some new, weird teaching. She told Mike Jesus Christ was coming back to earth. He had laughed in derision and told his wife that if, indeed, Jesus did make another appearance it would make a whale of a newsstory.

Mike glanced over at the AP machine. *Wouldn't that be something?* He chuckled to himself. *I can just see it,* he thought:

AP38490—(New York)—A spokesman for the United Nations told representatives of the General Assembly today that Jesus Christ had requested permission to address them at tomorrow's session. He confirmed that it was the same Jesus Christ who had lived and died in Palestine nearly 2,000 years ago. The spokesman said that permission had been denied. The appearance of Christ in the General Assembly would provoke a storm of protest from the Soviet bloc. He also indicated that several New York clergymen denied that it was possible for this to be Christ, that he had been buried and was quite dead.

"Dead is right!" muttered Mason. "And my wife is following a dead man along with the rest of those nuthouse refugees. All those fanatics and their wacko followers—now my wife becomes a religious nut!"

"Mike, what's happening?" Sally Tamm walked into the newsroom. "Anything breaking on the teacher strike?"

Mason draped his feet over the typewriter stand. "Sally, I want to ask you something. What would you say if I told you Jesus Christ had returned to earth?"

The tall brunette looked at him and laughed, "I would say you had been hitting the sauce again."

"Yeah. You're right. Only a wino would believe that story. Well, it was just a wild thing that went through my mind. Yell at the crew, will you? And let's get the show on the road."

Motorists could not help noticing the attractive young girl speeding south on Third Avenue. The top was down on her late model MG and her long blond hair was even more beautiful blowing in the wind. Oversized dark glasses hid her steel-gray eyes.

Patricia Stallings, 19, was in a hurry—not only today, but throughout her entire life. Her exceptional mind had allowed her to graduate from McKinley High School at 15 and from State College 3 years later. None of her friends doubted that Pat would succeed in life. And already she showed early returns on that prediction. Following a lead on a job, she had applied for a spot as an assistant buyer for Gamble's Department Store. Her charm and rather startling perception got her by the dubious placement officer and onto the payroll. At 19 she was making more money than her father who was 46.

Pat frowned as she thought about her dad. The one flaw in her blossoming life was her relationship with her parents. James Stallings was completing his 25th year on the production line at Ford Motor Company. He had no ideas about climbing much higher and it didn't bother him. His wife Martha was still attractive and remained content in her role as a homemaker.

Pat and her parents would have been quite compatible if it were not for their religion. They were members of Christian Assembly—and had been as long as Pat could remember. The church was a nondescript little brick building in a nonprogressive part of the city. The pastor, Fred Shelton, had filled the structure many times, but rather than relocate or add onto the existing building, he had insisted on starting another church. So Christian Assembly had "mothered" six churches in the area.

That was one of the things that upset Pat about the place. Why not move out to the suburbs—build a cathedral-like church in keeping with today's society? One where you would be proud to bring your friends? Pat would have taken a physical beating before bringing any of her friends to that broken-down old building.

But it was far more than the structure that upset her and caused her to leave the church. It was the strange teachings. The pastor taught—and her parents sincerely believed—that Jesus Christ had risen from the dead 3 days after his execution at Calvary. He taught that it was possible for sick bodies to be supernaturally healed by this "resurrected" Christ, and that a person could be "filled with the Holy Spirit" and speak in a strange, unlearned language. But the weirdest doctrine of all to Pat was their teaching about the return of Christ. Her parents believed Christ would set up a world government and rule the earth for 1,000 years. But before He did that they believed He would secretly catch away all His followers to a "marriage supper." To Pat's mind it all smacked of superstition. She totally rejected such things.

Her life-style would not permit such foolishness either. Her parents' church taught that a person should live within holy guidelines set forth in the Bible. But Pat had long since joined the free and easy living of her peers. Her roommate for the past 6 months had been Guy Jerrod. She had met him on a skiing weekend. There was a magnetism the first time their eyes met. Within a week Pat had begun living with Guy, although she knew her parents were brokenhearted about it.

Her relationship with her folks was important to Pat, however. If only they would understand that times changed, people changed, customs changed. You couldn't live in a box all your life—a box nailed shut by all the weirdos who came along. She didn't try to influence others to live as she did. Why wouldn't people give her the same consideration?

In desperation she called her folks to have dinner with her. Her mother, Martha, insisted Pat come home and join them for a home-cooked meal. Pat had to admit it wasn't a bad idea. She was getting tired of restaurants. So the date was set and this was the night of the get-together.

Pat wheeled the convertible onto a side road and into the old familiar neighborhood. The junior high school set back in the trees brought her a wave of memories, most of them unpleasant. It was in the third floor girls' room where she had experimented for the first time with pot. The experimentation had long since become a way of living.

Turning onto her parents' street, Pat hoped the meal would be a pleasant one, without any bickering. She decided not to bring up anything controversial and to be as agreeable as possible.

Her dad's station wagon was in the driveway. Apparently he had been giving it a needed wash job. The hose was still running, pouring water down the driveway, and the sponge was resting on the hood of the car. But her father was nowhere in sight. Perhaps the telephone had taken him away for a moment.

Pat walked around the corner of the house and turned the faucet off. Strange that he had left the water running like that. One of the things he had drummed into her was economy. It wasn't like him to leave the hose on.

Running up the front steps, Pat wished again that her folks would have permitted Guy to come with her. He was so good looking, and what a charmer! If they would only sit down with him, they would easily understand why Pat was living with him. But they wouldn't even meet him.

She pushed open the front door. "Mom... Dad... I'm here." There was no answer. Pat walked briskly into the living room and kitchen. She could smell the cooking food. She never had learned to cook like her mom. "Mother! Are you in here?" Still no answer. She noticed that food was boiling over onto the stove. The dinner rolls were burning in the oven. A dish lay shattered on the kitchen floor, the vegetables splashed everywhere.

"Mother!" What was happening here? Pat had never known her mother to do something like this.

She quickly turned off the stove and walked into the family room. It was empty. She ran up the steps to the bedrooms. Nobody there. Panic began to set in as Pat flew down the steps into the basement. It was empty too. The house was totally deserted.

But what could have happened? The running hose? The sponge on the hood of the car? The burning food? The broken dish on the kitchen floor? The empty rooms? Had they been kidnapped?

A thought suddenly struck her. "Oh, my God! Could it be that Christ really had come?"

She quickly dismissed that nonsense from her mind. No, there had to be a rational explanation for this. She called her apartment and told Guy what had happened. He promised to be right over.

Pat retraced her steps again. "Mom. . . Dad. . . is this a joke? Where are you? The fun's over! Please! Where are you?"

Perspiration beaded her brow. There was a catch in her throat as she picked up the telephone and dialed 911.

"Hello, police department? I want to report an emergency. My parents have disappeared. Simply vanished. Please come over and help me. . . ."

Mike Mason leaned back in his chair and put his feet on the desk. Director Terry Michaelson and two cameramen joined Mason's on-the-air staff. There were 2 hours until air time and several problems remained to be solved.

Larry Conners was the last one to arrive. No one needed to ask why. They knew he had been drinking his supper somewhere. But he looked okay so no one bothered him about it. Mason wondered to himself how soon it would be before Conners passed out on camera, probably sliding right down the weather board. The end of the weatherman's career was coming quickly; there wasn't much doubt about that.

"Okay, Mike. We're all here. Let's get started."

Mason glanced up at Sally Tamm. His co-anchor had changed into a soft, pastel-blue dress that clung tightly to her body. Mike knew she didn't dress provocatively on purpose. It was just that no matter what she wore she was gorgeous. He also knew that the thoughts he allowed to tramp through his mind night after night were becoming part of a pattern, a dangerous pattern. There was only one way it could go if he didn't change it. He wondered what would happen if he told Sally his thoughts. Would she respond?

If only Virginia hadn't gotten involved with those spiritual crackpots. He had never given Sally a second glance until recently. He knew he had to get a check on himself right away. The front office boys came down hard on employees who got involved in affairs. And he didn't really want an affair with Sally. Somehow he would have to get Virginia out of that religious web. Things would settle down to normal then.

"Terry, we need 40 seconds of video on the teacher strike. We'll pick up the audio where Superintendent Morrison gives the wage demands. Okay?"

"Yeah, Mike. No problem. At least I don't think so. I can't find Pete anywhere. Have any of you seen him?"

Pete Phillips was the new videotape man. Everyone agreed that he was the best they had ever had. But he was a bit strange at times—shy, quiet. Mason had entered Pete's office without knocking several days before and found him reading a Bible.

Pete's predecessor had left a stack of "skin" magazines in his desk, but they were no longer there. Phillips had cleaned them out and burned them before anyone had a chance to claim them.

Mason figured Pete was into the same thing as Virginia. But he never talked to him about it. One nut per person was sufficient.

Johnny Delbert was the last one who had seen Pete. "Yeah, I saw him about 20 minutes ago. Everything seemed okay then. Haven't seen him since."

Mason was beginning a slow burn. "Well, somebody find him and get him in here. We have a show to do. Next time he's late like this he can just keep going—to another job. Larry, anything special on the weather tonight?"

"Naw. Same as at 6. I'll need my usual 4 minutes. Might want to watch the radar in the northwest though. Accu-Weather said something could develop in that front. Seems like an unusual formation for this time of the year."

"Okay, Larry. Thanks. Johnny, it's a slow night in sports. Can we have about 30 seconds of your time? I'd like to do that bit on the truck accident again."

Delbert turned down the radio. He was listening to the fourth inning of the Mets game. "No problem, Mike. Pretty dull here."

"Okay then. Let's get to work. Terry, let me know when you find Pete. I want to talk to him. He's never missed a meeting before. He oughta know better than that."

Mason inserted some paper into his typewriter. It was five-ply with carbons between each sheet. The white copy went to the teleprompter operator; he kept the pink one; the yellow one went to Sally; the blue copy to Terry; and the green copy went in the permanent file.

Behind him the police radio came on. "Report to

1879 Crescent Drive. We have a missing couple. A Mr. and Mrs. James Stallings have reportedly disappeared. . . ."

Mason chewed on a nail for a moment. "Strange. Wonder what happened. And I wonder what's happened to Pete?"

The Rev. Ivar Johnson sat back in his reclining chair and yawned. It had been a long day. He was anxious for his wife Irene to pick him up. They were to meet Bishop Carlin for dinner at the country club.

Johnson glanced about his office contentedly. Not yet 50, he had reached the pinnacle of success in his ministry. He had been appointed senior pastor of First Church on his 46th birthday. Few doubted that he would succeed the bishop upon the latter's retirement.

The minister's office had been designed by the city's finest interior decorator. His library was the envy of his peers. Over 7,000 volumes graced the bookshelves, many of them first-editions and leatherbound. His collection of classics and 19th-century sermons was unsurpassed. His insurance agent had put a value on the collection of well over $80,000.

Johnson chuckled as he reflected on the long, tedious road he had climbed since seminary. Before finishing his second year of training he had ditched all vestiges of fundamentalism. The Virgin Birth, the return of Christ, the Blood atonement—all such teachings were throwbacks to the Middle Ages as far as he was concerned. And, he noted with satisfaction, most of those Bible-thumpers who held such archaic notions were still out in the boondocks trying to hold their tiny churches together.

Everything was satisfactory at First Church. Not only was it the most prestigious church in the city, but it boasted the finest architecture and furnishings. The tourist brochure printed by the Chamber of Commerce included the picture of only one church—his. No others were deemed worthy. The minister couldn't help laughing when he recalled the reaction of his friend Jim Maline, pastor of nearby Calvary Temple. Maline thought Calvary Temple should have been included too!

People considered their friendship incongruous — Ivar Johnson, minister *extraordinaire,* and Jim Maline, leader of the city's evangelicals. But Johnson realized what others did not, that Maline was a highly capable leader and a brilliant speaker. Johnson admitted that Maline's antique philosophies upset him at times, but he admired the work his friend had done in such a short time. When Maline began pastoring at Calvary Temple, it was a run-down congregation, barely able to meet its financial obligations. But in 3 short years the church had increased 500 percent and was continually building to keep up with the growth.

Ivar Johnson had met the evangelical preacher on the golf course, of all places. Johnson was proud of his 3 handicap; it was good enough to beat most golfers in the city—especially on the extremely long 6,900-yard Pinecrest Club. But he could only edge Maline about a fourth of the time. He knew Maline thrived on beating him.

The two friends had carried on long debates in the clubhouse following their donnybrooks on the golf course. Jim Maline, charismatic; Ivar Johnson, modernist. It made for stimulating discussion. It had bothered Johnson when his wife Irene attended several of the ladies' weekday sessions at Calvary Temple. She never said much about them, but there were certain discernible changes in her behavior. For example, Ivar had walked into his study in the manse on more than one occasion to find his wife praying. It was not a recited prayer; it was impassioned and fervent. And she began wanting to discuss his Sunday morning sermons. Irene had never been interested in that before. Her questions were irritating.

"Ivar, darling, how do you know Jesus Christ was not resurrected? It seems to me the evidence is far more on the evangelical side of the question than your position. What happened to His body? Who would have taken it? And for what reason?"

"Irene, don't fall into the old debate trap. There is simply no scientific explanation for such a phenomenon as resurrection. You surely can't accept such an outrageous conclusion without any backing."

"But, Ivar, there are absolute proofs that. . . ."

"Irene, I don't want to discuss it. The whole thing is passe′. Forget it."

At times the Rev. Johnson could be cutting and carnal. He hated himself for it—but Irene should know better than to be so pedantic. She had never been to Bible college, let alone seminary.

He was grateful that his wife had let up on him in recent weeks. It wasn't that she had quit the weekday sessions or that she prayed and studied less. She was still totally involved. (And it upset him when Irene offered some of her evangelical learnings in her Sunday school class.) But at least she wasn't cornering him anymore. He was relieved. Their discussions had been terribly unnerving.

Johnson suddenly sat up in his chair. Where was Irene, by the way? He had been lost in his reverie for more than 40 minutes. His wife had been due at the church much earlier. He picked up the phone and dialed their home number. No answer. *At least,* he thought, *she is on her way.*

While he was waiting, he decided to call Maline and confirm their golf match for Saturday. He was looking forward to the game more than he wanted to admit. But there was no answer at the charismatic preacher's home either.

Johnson leaned back in the recliner to wait for his wife. Idly, he picked up a copy of a magazine he had received in the mail that afternoon and began reading the lead story: "Millions of people around the world believe that Jesus Christ will someday return to this planet. . . ."

Mack Thomlin leaned back in the passenger seat of the late model Chevy and began to doze. He had hitchhiked all the way across the country. Leaving San Francisco 4 days earlier, he was on his way to Boston. Not much of the journey remained, and he was grateful for the driver who had just picked him up.

"What's your name, young fella?" Thomlin had nearly fallen asleep when the driver began the conversation. Mack hoped he could end it fast; he desperately needed the rest.

"Ah, Thomlin—Mack Thomlin. I'm headed for

Boston. That's my home. Left there several years back to complete my education in California."

"That so? What was your major?"

Thomlin silently cursed under his breath. Just his luck to get a gabby driver. "English. I've done some writing—in fact, I sold a couple of pieces already. I needed some polishing in several skills, so that's the reason for the education. Degree didn't mean so much as the tools, you know?"

The driver pulled a paperback from behind the sun visor and tossed it to his passenger. "My name's George Lackman. I live fairly close to Boston. I'll get you most of the way home. Say, did you ever read that book?"

Thomlin looked at the slim volume. It had a nondescript, dark illustration on the cover. The title was *The God Who Is There* and it was written by a Francis A. Schaeffer.

"What's this, Mr. Lackman?"

"Well, I thought you might find it intriguing. Schaeffer is one of our finest contemporary philosophers. In this book he deals with the modern relevance of Christianity." Mack reacted quickly.

"It doesn't have any relevance!"

"What do you mean by that?" asked Lackman.

"Christianity is dead, man. It's been dead for a long time—and for some of us it was never alive. I belong to the school of rationalism. No one has ever proved that God exists; therefore, the very thought that He does is an affront to my rational mind. I don't buy anything that can't be proved."

Lackman chuckled. "Sounds to me like you're involved with the New American Library folks in New York."

Thomlin showed his surprise. "How do you know about that?"

"Well, my young friend, I have read every book and essay that Ayn Rand ever wrote. She's quite an interesting person. I find some truths in her theories of objectivism and self-interest; however, her denial of the very God who gave her life is not reasonable."

Thomlin was thoroughly taken aback. "You mean you are well read on some of our modern philosophy and you still involve yourself with religion? You know that God never has existed. No one can deny that rationally. I suppose Thomas Aquinas came as close as anyone to proving God through philosophy. But even he failed. There's no way, man—no way a sane person can believe in God."

Lackman looked away from his driving for a moment to study his passenger's face. He was so young—and already a cynic. As he turned his attention back to the highway, Lackman breathed a prayer for guidance to deal successfully with the disbeliever.

"Mack, I cannot prove to you in a few minutes here in this car that there is a God. I can only tell you that over 25 years ago I found the reality of His being. You know, man must have hope. You just can't plod along through life knowing that the grave is the end of the line. I have enjoyed this life tremendously. But I know this is only the beginning of the way. I believe in eternity and I am certain that Jesus Christ gives me access to eternal life. Here, let me give you some reasons. . . .

Sensing no reaction, the driver glanced toward his passenger. Mack Thomlin was so tired that he hadn't stayed in the discussion. He had leaned his head against the car window and fallen asleep.

Lackman breathed a prayer, "Well, Lord, let me be prepared when he wakes up. Maybe there'll be a new name written in heaven today."

The Chevrolet hit the sharp curve at 57 miles an hour. The great weight of the full-size car broke easily through the restraining cable. It began plunging down the embankment. Thomlin woke up with a scream as he saw a row of trees suddenly appear before the careening car. He turned toward the driver to register his panic.

But when he looked at the driver's side he experienced still greater fear. It was unbelievable! Totally irrational! The driver's door was still closed, locked, and the window was intact. But Lackman was gone. The man had completely disappeared. There was no one there! But . . . how . . . ?

Confusion was the last thing that registered in young Thomlin's brain before his body was torn to pieces in the screaming, tearing wreck.

Josh Taggart settled into a recliner chair to read the evening paper. He placed his very dry martini—the third one of the evening—on the tray beside the chair, and pulled the footrest to its highest position. He couldn't remember when he had felt so tired. In the 13 years he had been news director at Channel 2 he had never felt more anxious to leave work and enjoy a night at home than he had today. His wife Ceil had left for the night with her bowling team. His teenage son, Joshua, was on a date somewhere. What more could a man ask for than such a serene evening?

He leaned over to the bookshelf and turned on the record changer. One of his favorite Davie Brubeck albums was already on the turntable. He placed the volume on low, pulled the paper in front of his face, and began working very hard at relaxing.

In the early days of television, the job of news director was much easier. All a person had to do was be a fairly good journalist and be able to read reasonably well. But the maturing of the medium brought with it rating points. Each point was worth a lot of money. Ratings were jacked up more by personalities than by responsible reporting. And the younger the personality, the better. So his work now turned more to the area of management than journalism.

Taggart was weary with it all. He had no idea what he was going to do with Larry Conners. The weatherman had been positively wobbly the night before. And the front office wanted some action on the problem before there was an on-camera disaster.

The news director yawned. "Tomorrow. Yeah, tomorrow. Let's fix it all tomorrow."

The incessant telephone broke into his reverie. Taggart wearily pulled himself from his chair and walked into the kitchen. The yellow wall phone continued ringing.

"Uh, hello, Taggart here."

"Josh? Josh? This is Mike Mason."

"Mason? What's the problem?" Warning bells went off in Josh's brain. Mason would not call this close to a newscast unless there was trouble.

"Josh, I need you down here. We've got big problems."

"Problems? Is it Conners? Did he show up drunk? This is the last. . . ."

"No, no, no. Man, I wish that was the problem. Josh, you better hang on to something. . . ."

Taggart exploded: "Come on, Mason! What is it?"

There was a slight pause. "Josh, it seems that several hundred people have disappeared from our city."

"Disappeared? You mean. . . left?"

"No—I mean disappeared. Vanished. Zappo. It's like they vanished in less than a second."

Taggart's mind was already working. "Okay, Mike, I'm coming. Who are these people? Any pattern?"

"Doesn't seem to be. Young, old. Various economic backgrounds. And they come from different neighborhoods. But I'll tell you this, Josh, the phones are ringing off the hooks. We got the switchboard operator back on duty tonight—which didn't make her very happy. And if you give me the okay, I'll call the whole news staff in. I think we're gonna have a long, long night."

"Yeah. Good thinking, Mike. Go ahead and tell 'em to come in. I'll be down in about 15 minutes. Better start throwing on some promo spots for the news."

"Good as done, Josh. See you in a few minutes."

Mason hung up, relieved that he had been able to get his director at that time of the night. He didn't want the responsibility for preempting *The Tonight Show* at 10:30. As he lit a cigarette and tried to get his thoughts together, a terrible pain suddenly began burning deep in his brain. He tried to reject it, but it grew faster and faster.

Involuntarily he moaned. Sports director Johnny Delbert heard it and looked up.

"Hey, Mike, you all right?"

"Oh, God, it can't be. I don't believe it. Gotta be some other explanation. That's just a fairy tale."

Memories of his arguments with Virginia began hurtling through his mind. She had told Mike of her belief in the return of Christ. She had said every living believer in Jesus would be instantly transported from earth into the air, to be with Him. And they would disappear for a short number of years while all hell broke loose on this planet.

Mike had laughed at her. Impossible. Can't happen! Only a fool could believe such a weird philosophy. But now—*maybe it is possible—maybe Christ . . . . How can I make sure?* Suddenly it dawned on him. There was one way to prove that this explanation was no good. He grabbed the phone and quickly punched the numbers connecting him with his house.

The connection was made and the phone began to ring.

"Come on, answer the telephone, Virginia!" he muttered.

But there was no answer and the phone continued to ring. He slammed down the receiver and threw the cigarette butt on the floor. *What was that preacher's name? Hennings. . . that was it.* He tore through the telephone directory and found the minister's number. He dialed it and waited. Again the phone rang and rang. No answer. He couldn't locate Virginia or the preacher. Who else could he contact? What other believers did he know? Ah! His neighbors. He dialed their number. No answer.

The awful truth was beginning to sink in on the Channel 2 anchorman. Beads of sweat broke out on his forehead. He felt like he needed to throw up.

Sally Tamm swept into the newsroom with another late report of missing persons. She glanced at her news partner. "Mike, Mike, what's the matter with you? You look like a dead man!"

Mason looked at her with dull eyes. "Sally, you hit the nail right on the head. I am a dead man. You're dead, too."

"Mike, have you flipped? What's the matter with you?"

"Dear Sally, tonight you and I are going to report the biggest story in the history of the world. I know where those people are who have disappeared. . . ."

All the staff members were in their places at 9:59 p.m. In the control room, director Terry Michaelson sat behind the huge console. Directly below him Marv Gannon hunched over the master control board. The projectionist was just completing a soap commercial. The station ID hit the screen and the 10 o'clock report was on live. VTR 3 rolled the opening theme and credits. The floor director cued Mike Mason onto camera 2. The newsman took a deep breath and began to read.

"Good evening. The world stopped for thousands of people in our city tonight. They simply vanished from this earth. It is a situation that is apparently worldwide. Following this newscast, *The Tonight Show* will be delayed 30 minutes so we may bring you the NBC report on the millions who have apparently vanished from every country.

"In our own city, there is panic everywhere. Police report rioting in the streets. It is as if there were no restraint left anywhere. Bars are packed. The sheriff's department has declared martial law.

"This is the strangest and saddest day in the history of mankind. Ladies and gentlemen, I have the story behind the story. Please listen carefully. I am going to tell you where your loved ones have disappeared. . . ."

# 2
# SIGNS

The chapter you have just read is, of course, fiction. One can only speculate on how the Rapture will transpire and its effect on individuals. There are those who believe that the missing saints will not be mourned once the restraint of the Holy Spirit is lifted from the earth. Who can say for sure? It is never safe to speculate beyond the dimensions set forth in Scripture.

My good friend, Evangelist David A. Lewis, well-known internationally for his prophetic discourses, has said that friends of prophecy have hurt the subject far more than its enemies. He means that those who have played such favorite games as "Name the Antichrist" and "Number, Number—Who's Got the Number?" (the number 666) do the cause of Christ no good. Candidates for "the Beast" form a long line from the days of Nero to the present. No one knows who the Antichrist will be anymore than anyone can pinpoint the day of Christ's return.

However, there are many signs that indicate that Christ's return for the Church is imminent. The 10 years I spent in the radio-television news business sharpened my senses to be on the alert for them.

I delivered my first radio newscast at age 17. Shortly thereafter, I crossed over to television. That was years before commercial color telecasting and the advent of videotape.

A microphone in my hand and a TV camera at my side opened the door to many people and places. For example, I covered 17 first-degree murder cases in my career. I interviewed most of those who stood trial. (The stiffest sentence I saw any of those individuals receive was 9 months. None of the accused men showed any inclination toward remorse.)

One afternoon the police radio led me to a remote street in our city. I arrived at the same time as law enforcement officials and the ambulance. Lying beside the front step of her home was a middle-aged lady who had been literally torn in two by a shotgun blast.

The man who had shot her had been involved in a card game. He had become enraged at what he considered cheating by the other players and had driven to his home for his shotgun. He was in a boiling rage when he came back and turned the gun on the players. The victim, who had not been involved in any of the proceedings, had inadvertently stepped from her front door and into the line of fire just as the trigger was pulled. She never knew what hit her.

Her body was picked up in two sections and taken to the morgue. An hour later I sat in the holding cell interviewing the accused killer. It was all a big joke to him. He chatted endlessly about everything except the tragic end to a human life.

During his trial his demeanor never changed. His first-degree charge was reduced to manslaughter and he received a 6-month sentence (despite the fact that it was the second time he had killed another human being).

The news business is a quick education in the course, "Man's Inhumanity to Man." I know of few reporters who would subscribe to the theory that the world is getting better and better. Whether they admit it or not, most newspeople would agree with God's assessment of mankind described in Romans:

> As it is written, There is none righteous, no, not one: there is none that understandeth, there is none that seeketh after God. They are all gone out of the way, they are together become unprofitable; there is none that doeth good, no, not one. Their throat is an open sepulchre; with their tongues they have used deceit; the poison of asps is under their lips: whose mouth is full of cursing and bitterness: their feet are swift to shed blood: destruction and misery are in their ways: and the way of peace have they not known: there is no fear of God before their eyes (Romans 3:10-18).

Day after day, pounding a news beat, a reporter becomes all too familiar with the sinful nature of mankind. Ask yourself, would you want to live in a city, such as Chicago or Los Angeles, if all the law enforcement officers were removed? It is hardly safe to walk the streets of many of our large cities—even in broad daylight—*with* police on duty. What would it be like if there were no authority at all? Would you want to stake your life on the innate goodness of mankind then?

Yet I remain an optimist! The future of the world is tremendous. An event is on the horizon that will trigger the countdown to the end of time and usher us into eternity with God.

That event is the rapture of the Church. Our Lord Jesus gave the world its greatest hope when He promised:

> Let not your heart be troubled: ye believe in God, believe also in me. In my Father's house are many mansions: if it were not so, I would have told you. I go to prepare a place for you. And if I go and prepare a place for you, I will come again, and receive you unto myself; that where I am, there ye may be also (John 14:1-3).

Man cannot live without hope. I have seen men die for no other reason than that they had abandoned all hope.

I was working the Saturday morning news shift for a radio station many years ago. The sheriff of our county called me and said he was passing the station en route to an emergency. He asked if I would like to go with him. I assured him that I would. I was very young and naive and not too familiar with proper police procedures.

We drove west of the city into a grove of trees, where we found an older model Ford parked near a fishing pond. I jumped from the patrol car and ran to the Ford, where I saw a man sitting in the passenger seat. I jerked open the door, not waiting for the sheriff. The man in the car was staring right at me. But he wasn't seeing anything.

He had sealed the windows of his car with masking tape and strung a hose from the exhaust system into the car itself. He had then tied himself securely to the passenger side and started the ignition, causing lethal fumes to pour into the cabin. Apparently to make sure he would die, he had taken a razor blade and slashed his wrists.

There was blood all over his body. And to make doubly sure he would die, he had filled the floor of the car with gasoline and there was a box of matches on his lap. I found the suicide note on the seat nearby, read it, and quickly passed it to the sheriff. It was the most gruesome message I have ever read. The law officer and I never revealed the contents of the note; protecting both the young man's memory and his family.

He had lost all hope. Life was useless to him. So he took the "easy" way out.

We receive letters constantly in our *Revivaltime* office from people who tell us that the radio message they heard about Christ changed their minds about suicide. Why? Because our message is one of hope. Christ can transform your life in this world. *Plus* He is coming again to reveal a whole new world.

Several years ago, the brilliant space scientist Dr. Wernher Von Braun appeared on a Christian television program. This genius, whose mind caused missiles to soar unerringly into outer space, told of the two greatest motivational forces in the world:

> I believe there are two forces which move us: one is a belief in a last judgment when everyone of us has to account for what we did with God's great gift of life on the earth. The other is belief in an immortal soul, a soul which will cherish the reward or suffer the penalty decreed in a final judgment.
>
> Science has found that nothing can disappear without a trace. Nature does not have extinction. All it knows is transformation. Benjamin Franklin, a scientist, put it well: "I believe that the soul of man is immortal and will be treated with justice in another life respecting its conduct in this." Everything science has taught me, and continues to teach me, strengthens my

belief in the continuity of our spiritual existence after death. Nothing disappears without a trace.

Many of the world's greatest people have zeroed in on the Rapture of the Church as the great hope of mankind. I love the story Dr. John Wesley White inserted in his book *Re-entry!* It concerns that legend of English history, Queen Victoria:

> Queen Victoria refused to break precedent with tradition and go to hear Spurgeon, a non-Anglican, expound, although her curiosity almost got the best of her on one or two occasions. But her Chaplain, Dean Farrar, was as passionate a believer in the second coming of Christ as Spurgeon, and so was Queen Victoria. On the first anniversary of the accession of Edward VII to the throne of England, during the service in Canterbury Cathedral, Dean Farrar finally revealed how the late Queen, after hearing one of her chaplains preach at Windsor on the second coming of Christ, spoke to the Dean about it and said, "Oh, how I wish that the Lord would come during my lifetime." "Why does your Majesty feel this very earnest desire?" asked the Dean. With appropriate emotion, she replied, "Because I should so love to lay my crown at His feet." *(Re-entry!* Zondervan Publishing House. Pages 23, 24.)

I share the same hope as Von Braun and Queen Victoria. And I know that I shall see them in glory some day. What greater message of victory and rejoicing could be shared with the world than this—Jesus is coming again? As an old (retired) newsman, my reasons for believing this truth are not just emotional, though there is tremendous emotion involved in it, of course. The reasons for my hope are logical and solid. I am convinced the next major event in God's prophetic plan is the rapture of the Church to meet Christ Jesus in the air.

# 3
# THE DISAPPEARANCE

For the Lord Himself shall descend from heaven with a shout, with the voice of the archangel, and with the trump of God: and the dead in Christ shall rise first: then we which are alive and remain shall be caught up together with them in the clouds, to meet the Lord in the air: and so shall we ever be with the Lord. Wherefore comfort one another with these words (1 Thessalonians 4:16-18).

It was the strangest afternoon of my career as a newscaster. I was enjoying a noon mealtime with my wife, preparing to leave for the radio station in a couple of hours. The telephone rang; it was my boss. He said, "Dan, there is a very important interview that has just come up; I want you to conduct it." He gave me 15 minutes to get there.

I reluctantly told my boss that I didn't think I could humanly make it in the time he prescribed. And I asked, "Who is to be interviewed anyway?"

My heart nearly stopped as he answered, "The President of the United States." There was a short pause. Then my response: "I'll be right there."

It is amazing how fast a person can move when he truly wants to. I arrived at the station, met one of the engineers in a mobile news unit, and we sailed down the highway to meet the president's caravan at a roadside park. Someone escorted me to the president's car and I was formally introduced. The interview began.

You must remember that a few moments before I had been home eating, unaware of anything special that day. And then—there he was! Two feet away! The President of the United States, Harry S. Truman.

It was a perfectly dreadful interview. I just wasn't ready for it. I couldn't think, the words wouldn't come out properly, the questions were not meaningful or important. It was a woeful exhibition. I just couldn't get ready to meet the president in 15 minutes. I don't really think many people could.

It makes the Biblical warning so shocking—we won't have 15 minutes to prepare to meet Jesus when He returns. We will have less than a second! Paul put it like this: "We shall all be changed, in a moment, in the twinkling of an eye, at the last trump" (1 Corinthians 15:51, 52). That is the time allotted for the greatest disappearance of humanity this world will ever know.

You see, there will be no time for preparation, no time for praying then, no time for setting things in order, no time for getting right with God. You will either be ready at that instant—or you will be left. Is it any wonder that God pleads with you, "Behold, now is the accepted time; behold, now is the day of salvation" (2 Corinthians 6:2)?

The Bible makes it clear that one day God will decide to bring His children home to himself. Jesus will break through the clouds with a shout of victory, the trumpet of God will alert every believer on this planet, and gravity will go into temporary suspension. Every man and woman who has committed his or her life to God and passed away on this earth will be taken first. "Then we which are alive and remain shall be caught up together with them in the clouds, to meet the Lord in the air" (1 Thessalonians 4:17). It will be a massive disappearance. The world will be stunned by it. Millions and millions of people will suddenly be gone.

Every race will be affected by it, every nation. Those who have disappeared will be from many different church denominations. They will be of all ages, various educational backgrounds, rich and poor. But there will be one common denominator among them all: sometime in their lives on this earth, they made the decision to commit their lives to Christ. They fulfilled that decision by praying to Almighty God to forgive their sins. They repented with all the fervency they possessed and they asked Jesus Christ to come into their hearts and lives. Then they began to live for the Lord every single day. And they looked for Jesus constantly.

So they were not shocked when the trumpet of God sounded, and the sky bleached white with the dazzling appearance of Jesus in the clouds. Their response was a joyful, "Even so, come Lord Jesus."

I want to share with you three basic reasons why I am convinced that Jesus will shortly return to this earth in the manner just described.

*First, Jesus said He would return.* Nearly everyone you meet will tell you that Jesus was the greatest person who ever lived. Any person receiving the accolades given to Jesus would have to be a person of virtue and truth. Jesus was such a man. And He spoke often of His return to receive His followers.

> But of that day and hour knoweth no man, no, not the angels of heaven, but my Father only. But as the days of Noah were, so shall also the coming of the Son of man be. . . . Watch therefore; for ye know not what hour your Lord doth come (Matthew 24:36, 37, 42).
>
> For the Son of man shall come in the glory of his Father with his angels; and then shall he render unto every man according to his deeds. Verily I say unto you, There are some of them that stand here, who shall in no wise taste of death, till they see the Son of man coming in his kingdom (Matthew 16:27, 28, *ASV*).

When our Lord ascended to His Father, the disciples were alone on top of Mt. Olivet and felt concern. Suddenly angels attended them and repeated Jesus' promise: "Ye men of Galilee, why stand ye gazing up into heaven? this same Jesus, which is taken up from you into heaven, shall so come in like manner as ye have seen him go into heaven" (Acts 1:11).

Jesus' words—on any subject—always comprised the mind of God revealed to man. Since God is perfect, Jesus' words were always true. If Jesus said—as He did so many times—that He would return for His followers and take them to be with Him forever, you can count on it! That revelation is direct from God to you. You can stake your life and soul on it!

When General MacArthur said, "I am going away, but I shall return," the American armies had lost their grip on Corregidor in the early part of World War II. The Allies had no future in the Pacific. Years later, MacArthur's armies marched down the shell-pocked streets of Manila, ending action in that theater of war. It was then that men remembered the general's boast. Every lip, newspaper, and radio affirmed, "General MacArthur has returned!"

Two thousand years ago, Jesus of Nazareth took a leave of absence from this planet. But before He left He said, "I will come again." And, my friend, as surely as MacArthur made good his declaration with the aid of land, sea, and air power, Jesus Christ—backed by the all-powerful hand of the Creator of the universe, flanked by legions of shining angels, and heralded by the tearing of the sky and blaring of trumpets—will someday return as He said. It will be the greatest story in history.

*Second, the validity of prophetic Scripture assures His return.* The Old Testament Scriptures regarding Christ's first coming were so numerous and detailed that the chances of their all coming true could not be coincidence. Someone has fed this information into a computer and come up with this figure: the odds of all the Old Testament prophecies regarding Jesus' birth coming true were one in 87 followed by 93 zeroes!

But here is the clincher: for every prophecy regarding Christ's first coming, there are two that tell us He is coming again! And the circumstances surrounding each of those Scripture passages are most remarkable. The Word of God is implicit on the theology of the return of Christ. The teaching of the return of our Lord is dealt with 1,845 times in the Bible; 318 of them in the New Testament. The coming of Christ is the dominant theme of 17 Old

Testament Books and one Epistle in the New Testament.

We are not talking about two or three isolated Scripture passages taken out of context; we are dealing with fully one-fourth of all Scripture. No other spiritual theme, besides redemption, is covered so thoroughly in your Bible. Yes, I am convinced that Jesus will return because of the prophetic part of God's Word that assures me of this blessed truth.

*Third, His return is the only hope this world has!* I have walked through rows of hundreds of men and women, virtual skeletons, lying in the dirt, dying of starvation. As we have given them bread, they have tugged at our clothing and, in their native tongue, have tried to thank us. Starvation is claiming its victims at an incredible rate.

The world is watching the Middle East. Will there be peace? Will the terrorist activities stop? Will the constant shelling of innocent persons end? Will the great cities such as Beirut and Tehran become safe? Will the insatiable appetite for weapons ever cease? Can anyone end the chaos that has haunted those countries for so many decades?

What about the dwindling supply of natural resources? Does anyone have a solution to skyrocketing inflation? Will the various races of man ever consider each other brothers instead of conquerors? Is there a solution to the increasing crime rate? Will it ever be safe to walk in the great cities of the Western world?

But Jesus said, "Let not your heart be troubled; I will come again!" I believe His words for a reason: every place His gospel has been accepted there has been new life and hope. Our democratic nations have been predicated on the Ten Commandments; they have given sanity to society. In every nation where Christianity has been abandoned, barbarism has reared its hideous head. Christ's gospel has given this world its finest literature, art, and music. His gospel has constantly opposed tyranny and the slavery of mankind. And when He returns, He will bring us an entirely new dimension of liberty and victory. He is our hope!

There is no question about it—Jesus will return. But there will not be 15 minutes' notice to get ready. He will come in an instant—in the twinkling of an eye.

# 4
# DIADEMS AND ASHES

A crucial question facing every born-again believer is: what happens to Christians following the rapture? We know the trump of God will sound and there will be a mass exodus from this earth of every living and dead saint. Where will we go? What activities will consume our next few years?

An observant person will notice that there is a vast variety among Christians. The apostle Paul wrote of four distinct types of believers in 2 Timothy:

"Demas hath forsaken me, having loved this present world.... Only Luke is with me. Take Mark, and bring him with thee: for he is profitable to me for the ministry.... Alexander the coppersmith did me much evil" (2 Timothy 4:10, 11, 14).

*Demas*—the lure of the world system got to him. Discipleship and cross bearing were not for him. When the going got tough, he left for greener pastures.

*Luke*—faithful, courageous Luke. We have no record of his forsaking the front line of ministry. He was instant in season and out of season. No matter what anyone else did, Luke could be counted on.

*Mark*—ran hot and cold. In his early years he had forsaken Paul and Barnabas to return home. But apparently something happened in his life to return him to his place as a soldier of Christ. He is a beautiful example of continuing faith in a person, even when that person has proven unprofitable for a time.

*Alexander*—he withstood Paul at every opportunity. How many there are who dress in saintly garb but are anything but saintly! Most Christian workers have come across the "Alexanders" in their lives.

These are four of the personality types you will meet in your endeavors for the Lord. There are obviously many more. What causes such a variety among believers?

Outside of Jesus, there has probably never been a more stalwart warrior of the Cross than the apostle Paul. His exploits for Christ are known throughout the world.

For many years I have been smitten by the life of this Spirit-energized man—so much so that several years ago I decided to retrace Paul's life from Tarsus, his birthplace, to his dungeon in Rome and execution spot on the Appian Way.

I was shocked during my visit to Tarsus. I found few Christians in the entire area. Strange that in the very birthplace of the first-century missionary-evangelist, little evangelism has occurred since. But in city after city I found evidences of the colossal witness of Paul.

I will never forget the morning I awoke in my cabin on a ship headed for Kavala, Greece. As I walked on the deck in the brilliant sunshine, I could see the city straight north of us about 10 miles. Kavala is a modern and extraordinarily beautiful city of about 65,000 persons. The Book of Acts refers to it as Neapolis.

Paul's first entrance into Europe was through this port city: "Therefore loosing from Troas, we came with a straight course to Samothracia, and the next day to Neapolis; and from thence to Philippi" (Acts 16:11, 12).

Kavala (or Neapolis) is situated on a steep mountainside that dips into the sparkling blue waters of the Aegean. On the north side of the mountain, lying in a magnificent valley, are the ruins of Philippi. Paul and Silas had a most unusual ministry there. Their first recorded European convert was Lydia, a business woman from Thyatira, who sold elegant fabrics in Philippi. The little creek where she and her family were baptized is nearly dry now. The amphitheater where Paul preached still stands. It is called Penetas and is in usable condition.

The two missionaries were cruelly beaten after casting a spirit of divination from a young lady who cried to them daily. And they were cast into prison, where they languished in extreme pain. Although most of that prison has long since been destroyed, the inner jail cell, where it is believed Paul and Silas were thrown, is still standing. There are marks on the rocky wall that show where their stocks were anchored. Below them a groove on the floor made its way to an underground cistern. It carried the blood and gore from broken and bleeding bodies. This was the place where Paul and Silas sang in the night.

What a wretched place! There is a plaque on the wall with the witness: "For to me to live is Christ"! What a colossal man of God Paul was!

In place after place I saw the same witness of history. What was the difference between Paul and Demas? Had they not met the same Christ? Had they not received the same baptism of fire? Perhaps. But Paul gives us the clue—the secret that apparently motivated him: "For we must all appear before the judgment seat of Christ; that every one may receive the things done in his body, according to that he hath done, whether it be good or bad" (2 Corinthians 5:10). *There is the accountability factor.*

Every believer will someday stand before a holy God to give an account for his or her Christian service. There will be no judgment for our lives prior to our conversion—"There is therefore now no condemnation to them which are in Christ Jesus, who walk not after the flesh, but after the Spirit" (Romans 8:1)—but there will be definite accountability for our lives thereafter. Paul referred to the event often.

After the rapture of the Church, we believers have a date with the eternal Auditor. We are going to give a stewardship report of our Christian living. Salvation is free, certainly. But the rewards are not! I have a feeling that many tears will be shed at the Judgment Seat.

Before getting into the details of that judgment, let's examine the reason for the event. What is the purpose for such a detailed examination of our service? There is another grand event awaiting us following the Rapture. It is the Marriage Supper of the Lamb: "Let us be glad and rejoice, *and give honor to him:* for the marriage of the Lamb is come, and *his wife hath made herself ready"* (Revelation 19:7).

The two italicized phrases are vital to understanding this event—"and give honor to him" and "his wife hath made herself ready." Scripture makes it clear that not all Christians will receive the same position at the Marriage Supper. Indeed, it may not be the happiest of occasions for those believers who have not shown careful discipleship.

To gain a better understanding of this Marriage Supper we have to leave the context of our concepts of marriage ceremonies. We are "westerners." But Jesus was an "easterner," an oriental. Palestine was a part of Asia Minor. And the customs of that part of the world were (and still are) quite different.

A few years ago, I was producing a television film in the old Philistine area of Gaza and the Mediterranean seacoast. I wanted some footage of activities that smacked of the customs of Jesus' day. My host indicated that we could probably come up with something in a little Arab village south of Gaza. He was right!

We spent a fascinating afternoon among some extremely pleasant people. As we approached the town square, I set up the camera to record an event I will never forget. The square was jammed with hundreds of Arab men and boys. They were dancing for all they were worth around an embarrassed-looking gentleman in the very center of the square. He was sitting on a forlorn donkey and holding a huge, multi-colored umbrella over his head, although it was not raining. The umbrella looked like those used by golfers in America.

As the camera was grinding away, I asked my host what was happening. He said, "You are filming a marriage ceremony. The man on the donkey is the groom." I stopped shooting immediately! I asked, "Where is the bride?" There wasn't a woman anywhere in sight. My friend informed me that the bride and her friends were not invited to this ceremony. They would come later.

Seeing my puzzlement, he laughed and explained, "You have to understand, my friend, that in this country, the marriage festivities are for the groom, not the bride. There is nothing allowed here to detract from *him*!"

Suddenly, truths regarding the Marriage Supper of the Lamb became very clear. Of course! The Marriage Supper will be for Christ ("and give honor to him"). Nothing will be allowed at that event that would distract one eye from His magnificent glory. Therefore, prior to the Marriage Supper, we must all appear before the judgment seat of Christ. It will be a time to check out the hope chest we have prepared on this earth.

Motivation for serving the Lord is the key here. It's the old question asked by every good newsman—"Why?" Why do we serve Jesus? Why do we witness? Why do we minister? Why do we sing in church choirs? Why do we teach Sunday school classes? Why do we tithe? Why do we do anything for the Lord at all? It will be amazing on that day to discover how much of our Christian lives we have lived for our own aggrandizement. Each Christian will be called to stand alone before the throne of God to give an accounting of his discipleship.

Sometimes, rather shallow theology crops up in the songs we sing. We are told in some songs that we will erupt in a cacophony of joy when we get to heaven. Maybe so—but it won't be immediate. Let's recall the apostle John's first glimpse of the holy Throne:

> And immediately I was in the Spirit: and, behold, a throne was set in heaven, and one sat on the throne. And he that sat was to look upon like a jasper and a sardine stone: and there was a rainbow round about the throne, in sight like unto an emerald. . . . And out of the throne proceeded lightnings and thunderings and voices: and there were seven lamps of fire burning before the throne, which are the seven Spirits of God. And before the throne there was a sea of glass like unto crystal.
>
> And in the midst of the throne, and round about the throne, were four beasts full of eyes before and behind. . . . And the four beasts had each of them six wings about him; and they were full of eyes within; and they rest not day and night, saying, Holy, holy, holy, Lord God Almighty, which was, and is, and is to come.
>
> And when those beasts give glory and honor and thanks to him that sat on the throne, who liveth for ever and ever, the four and twenty elders fall down before him that sat on the throne, and worship him that liveth for ever and ever, and cast their crowns before the throne, saying, Thou art worthy, O Lord, to receive glory and honor and power: for thou hast created all things, and for thy pleasure they are and were created (Revelation 4:2, 3, 5, 6, 8-11).

This is not the place where we will "sing and shout and dance about." Great rejoicing and singing will come later. But at His throne there is an awesome awareness of the holiness of the

Creator. Contemporary Christianity has lost sight of much of the resplendent glory of God. His majesty has been replaced by altogether uninspired familiarity—"The Man Upstairs" concept. The late A.W. Tozer wrote:

> But the God we must see is not the utilitarian God who is having such a run of popularity today, whose chief claim to men's attention is His ability to bring them success in their various undertakings and who for that reason is being cajoled and flattered by everyone who wants a favor. The God we must learn to know is the Majesty in the heavens, God the Father Almighty, Maker of heaven and earth, the only wise God our Saviour. He it is that sitteth upon the circle of the earth, who stretcheth out the heavens as a curtain and spreadeth them out as a tent to dwell in, who bringeth out His starry host by number and calleth them all by name through the greatness of His power, who seeth the works of man as vanity, who putteth no confidence in princes and asks no counsel of kings. *(The Knowledge of the Holy.* Harper & Row, Publishers. Pages 121, 122.)

This is the God with whom we will have to deal at the Judgment Seat. Each of us will stand alone before Him, in full view of the saints of all ages. There will be nothing secret about the report. It will be shown to all. The rules of the judgment are devastating:

> But let every man take heed how he buildeth thereupon. For other foundation can no man lay than that is laid, which is Jesus Christ. Now if any man build upon this foundation gold, silver, precious stones, wood, hay, stubble; *every man's work shall be made manifest:* for the day shall declare it, because it shall be revealed by fire; and the fire shall try every man's work of what sort it is. . . . If any man's work shall be burned, he shall suffer loss: but he himself shall be saved; yet so as by fire (1 Corinthians 3:10-13, 15).

We have the option of using our life in any of six categories: gold, silver, and precious stones—all of which are precious, rare, and hard to find; or hay, wood, and stubble—all of which are common and in full sight of men. When fire is applied to gold, silver, and precious stones, it is a refining agent, leaving them purer and more precious than before. When fire is applied to hay, wood, and stubble, it leaves only ashes.

My dear friend Leonard Ravenhill has likened the gold to our love life with Jesus, our adoration and worship of Him; the silver to our works; and the precious stones to our prayer life. All three of those activities are very hard to find among the less devoted saints. The underground activity, the intercession that few people ever see, the giving to Christ that is not motivated by a tax exemption, the hidden eternal works, are sometimes hard to uncover.

When I first entered the ministry, I served as an assistant pastor. On our first Sunday there, I was intrigued by the activities of the church organist. There was not much positive to observe: she arrived late, her attitude was one of constant hostility, and her playing did nothing to enhance a worshipful attitude. I watched the same enactment week after week. I asked the pastor why the woman was tolerated in such a key position. He informed me that she was a "pillar," she had been the organist for 20 years—and she had the only key to the organ, which she was not about to relinquish.

In all probability, that woman will someday stand before the Judgment Seat. Every eye will be focused on the confrontation. I believe God will ask her, "________________, do you have anything to declare by way of service since your conversion?" She will answer, "Oh, yes! For 20 years I was the organist at First Church. Why, I never missed a Sunday. I was there rain or shine."

Then God will ask her, "Tell me—*why* were you the church organist? What motivated your playing?"

It will be impossible to fabricate stories on that day. Before assembled millions of saints, hundreds of thousands of angels, and the penetrating eyes of God himself, she will have to answer: "I did it for my own gratification. I didn't want anyone else to play the organ. I wouldn't have relinquished that public position for anything. It was my job!"

Then those 20 years of service will be taken to the flaming altar and placed on the coals. Was her playing gold? silver? precious stones? Those 20 years will go up in smoke. They were hay, wood, and stubble. All that remains will be ashes.

The rewards we lay at Jesus' feet will be the residue of that fire. The old song asks the question correctly: "Will there be any stars in my crown?" Another verse might ask: "Or will I have only handfuls of charred ashes?"

Each of us must grapple with this issue. Not only the *fact* of our service is vital; perhaps even more relevant is the *why* of our service. Each of us ministers must honestly answer the question: why do we preach? It is certainly an honor. Week after week, perhaps hundreds of people sit patiently listening to us. It is without question a position of dignity. What motivates us in this pursuit? Can we honestly say we want the mind of Christ each time we enter the pulpit? That we are aware of the tremendous, eternal issues at hand? That we want the beauty of Jesus to be seen in us?

Have you ever heard a singer introduce his song in church with this pathetic line: "Please pray for me as I try to sing this song. You know, I haven't had much time to practice, so you pray!" How awful! What an affront to Christ! Could you imagine Frank Sinatra standing before a crowd at Madison Square Garden and saying, "This song might not be very good. I've just been so busy that. . ."? Not in a million years!

You might respond, "Yes, but look how much Sinatra gets paid for his songs." Good point. Let's compare it with the reward you will get for faithful, properly motivated service to the King of kings. Sinatra is a pauper compared to you. Here is the question: why do *you* sing in church?

I have often heard choir members approach the minister of music to ask for a special solo part in a cantata, or the privilege of singing a solo in church. There is nothing wrong with that, provided the motivation is right. The ministry of music within the confines of a church service must never be a recital. It is not a concert. It is a ministry to God and nothing else. Every gospel singer will account for this very thing at the judgment seat of Christ.

Sunday school teacher—why do you hold forth each Lord's Day morning? What would your reaction be if the superintendent came to you and said, "I feel that perhaps we should give this class to Brother so and so." Would you be angry? Then ask yourself this: Why were you teaching that class in the first place? For yourself? Or for the kingdom of God? If the superintendent honestly felt the Kingdom could be enhanced by someone else's teaching, why should you be hurt by it if your motivation is correct?

I once held a meeting in a church where a building program was underway. One of the ladies had painted the nursery pink. Another lady didn't like pink so she came in, quite uninvited, and painted it blue. When the first lady saw what had happened she was terribly upset. And, of course, she returned with her bucket of pink paint and returned the nursery to its "proper" color. Then the second lady returned and. . . . I couldn't help wondering as I saw this overpainted room, would the ladies someday be singing, "A tent or a cottage, why should I care, as long as the church nursery is pink over there. . . "?

Ah, what hidden secrets will be publicly revealed on that wondrous day when we stand before Him! We may find that those heroes of the faith who command the spotlight in our day will not rate much attention at the Judgment Seat. On the other hand, little-known saints who never set foot on a platform, but who spent long and sleepless nights on their knees in intercession, will receive the highest honors of all.

I have tried to visualize the chronology of the events of that day. I cannot do more than imagine, of course. But there are certain things I know for sure. For example, I would not want to follow Paul's appearance at the judgment seat of Christ. Can you imagine it?

What a television spectacular Paul's appearance would make. Various authors have sought to describe him. Some things are known about him: he was relatively small; some believe his body was slightly deformed; others claim his eyesight was poor. He probably had a disappointing physical appearance. But there is so much more to a man than that. One author wrote that he believes Paul walked with a "holy swagger"! He certainly was no shrinking violet. "I can do all things through Christ. . . ," and, "I have fought a good fight."

Imagine that breathtaking moment when a mighty angel ascends an eternal battlement and, in a voice that would make worlds tremble, cries, "Saul of Tarsus, also known as Paul the Apostle!" From the immense crowd steps the man who caused mighty monarchs to shake. He confidently makes his way to the shimmering Throne and the presence of his God. "Here! I am here!" I believe there will be a delay in the proceedings while generations of believers stand to applaud this incredible man.

God speaks: "Paul, my Son Jesus appeared to you on the road to Damascus. You spent the remainder of your earthly life in His service. It is time for an accounting. What do you have to declare?"

Paul will begin the long list of triumphs. "Yes, Jesus was seen of me, 'as of one born out of due time. For I am the least of the apostles, that am not meet to be called an apostle, because I persecuted the church of God. But by the grace of God I am what I am: and his grace which was bestowed upon me was not in vain; but I labored more abundantly than they all: yet not I, but the grace of God which was with me' " (see 1 Corinthians 15:8-10).

One by one Paul will place major world cities he "conquered" for Christ before the Throne—Corinth, Thessalonica, Ephesus, and Antioch. One by one he will recount the dramatic stories of their being reached with the gospel in his lifetime. Each story is packed with tension and each made its mark on Paul's body. Those victories were not won without conflict and pain.

There is a tendency to imagine the cities Paul visited as "wide spots" in the road. Not so! Philippi was a major city, located on the main road between Rome and Istanbul. Ephesus was a city of vast dimension. I have visited the excavations of that western Turkish metropolis. I was stunned by what I saw, and my admiration for the apostle was heightened even more.

Ephesus in Paul's day was one of the three most important cities of the East. Alexandria of Egypt and Antioch of Syria were the others. It was the largest city of its time, boasting art galleries, gymnasiums, baths, marketplaces, theaters, and separate quarters for Egyptians, Greeks, Jews, and Syrians. Ephesus was a lively tourist and commercial center. Flocks of goats, sheep, and multitudes of people dressed in a variety of gaily colored apparel jammed the marble streets. Donkey, camel, and mule caravans brought European and Oriental wares.

The city was most famous for its Temple of Diana, one of the ancient Seven Wonders of the World. One month of every year was devoted to the worship of this goddess. No work was done, as the Ephesians flocked to the stadium to see races or games, watched plays in the theater, or sat enraptured by the musical concerts.

The Temple of Diana was an incredible structure, four times larger than the Parthenon. According to Pliny, it took 200 years to build it and contributions came from all over Asia. The building was 425 feet long and 225 feet wide. It had 127 columns, 60 feet high and 6 feet in diameter, each representing a king. Virtually nothing remains of the temple at its original site. What is left may be seen at the British Museum.

Paul's ministry in Ephesus played havoc with the worship of the phony goddess. His preaching hurt hell's business there. Statues of Diana became less in demand, and Satan's apostles decided to make war on God's apostle.

The confrontation, according to Acts 19, took place in the huge amphitheater. The place still exists and is still usable. It seats 25,000 persons. It was packed on the day Demetrius, the silversmith, called the workers together. For 2 hours they cried out, "Great is Diana of the Ephesians"! (See Acts 19:23-41.)

Paul shook the very foundations of hell in that pagan city. He made more of an impact on it than Anthony and Cleopatra.

Think of it! With no advance man, no modern media facilities, no sound systems, no Madison Avenue techniques—with nothing but the power of God, Paul shook the work of Satan in Ephesus. The citizens of that ancient metropolis could not withstand him. At tremendous danger to himself, the apostle fervently ministered through the power of the Holy Spirit.

Now he stands before God at the Judgment Seat. "What do I have to declare? Here is Ephesus! Here is Philippi, where Silas and I were beaten and thrown into prison. Here is Corinth, where I didn't make enough money to live on so I worked fulltime in order to exist. Here is Nero's dungeon where I languished the last years of my life before my execution. Here is my very life which I offered to Your service. I declare that my entire life, after I met Jesus on the road to Damascus, was lived in conquering the world for Him."

The assembled saints are hushed by this remarkable testimony. The next question from the Father will be the crucial test. "Paul, why did you so live? What motivated you in your pursuits? What did you hope to gain by it all?"

The apostle stands as straight as he can to deliver his answer. "Holy Father, I told the Christians in Corinth the answer to that question long ago: 'We have this treasure in earthen vessels, that the excellency of the power may be of God, and not of us. We are troubled on every side, yet not distressed; we are perplexed, but not in despair; persecuted, but not forsaken; cast down, but not destroyed; always bearing about in the body the dying of the Lord Jesus, *that the life also of Jesus might be made manifest in our body*' " (2 Corinthians 4:7-10).

There is the whole point of the test at the Judgment Seat. Can every believer say to God that he lived so the life of Jesus could be made manifest in his body? It is the only motivation that will have merit on that day.

Now we watch together as the great accumulation of Paul's works is taken to the raging fire of judgment. Will they be consumed; revealing them as nothing more than hay, wood, and stubble? Or will a brighter glow come from the blaze; indicating that gold, silver, and precious stones are being refined in that eternal heat?

Paul never once doubted on this earth what the answer would be. He testified that he expected a crown. He was confident of the outcome. Why? He never lost sight of that haunting reality: "For we must all appear before the judgment seat of Christ." He left nothing in his life to speculation.

Now angels gather around him to heap on him great rewards. But their glow is paled by the reflection from the face of the old apostle. Everything he suffered has now become abundantly worthwhile. All of heaven applauds. The saints of the centuries thunder their ovation. Paul has triumphed.

Now I ask you—how would you like to follow Paul to the Judgment Seat? Someone will. Do you begin to see the tremendous urgency of this moment?

Ah, but there is an even greater one to follow. The Marriage Supper of our Lord Jesus comes next. Remember nothing will be allowed in that place to detract from His presence. We will have the glorious opportunity to stand before Him, to touch those precious hands, to gaze into those loving eyes. And that will be our chance to lay our crowns at His feet.

Can you see Paul as he places at those nail-pierced feet the heaping rewards of his labor? Look at the dazzling gold and silver and precious stones. See the pride on the Saviour's face as He lifts Paul to embrace him. Paul foresaw this moment long ago: "For I reckon that the sufferings of this present time are not worthy to be compared with the glory" (Romans 8:18).

Now, it is your turn. You are summoned to the presence of Jesus Christ. Like Thomas long before, you are able actually to touch the One you have served. You kneel before Him. He is so altogether lovely, more magnificent than you have dared dream. You feel His hands lifting you to your feet. You look into those eyes. It is time for your presentation. What was left from the fire? Will you have many rewards and crowns to lay at His feet?

Or, will there come from your shaking hands... only the flow of ashes? Imagine it, if you will. Your great moment before the Son. And you have nothing prepared for it. Just... ashes....

# 5
# MEANWHILE, BACK ON EARTH. . .

No one can accurately predict when Jesus will take His bride away (the event we call the Rapture). It could well happen before you finish reading this book; it might not occur in your lifetime. However, anyone who is aware of the world situation knows a global government is no longer a far-fetched concept. During the 7-year span on earth following the Rapture, a world government will come into being, headed by Satan's masterpiece of deception, the Antichrist (a substitute messiah).

Twenty-five years ago, most people considered a world government impossible. Nationalism was still in vogue. The Korean and Vietnam conflicts have done much to curb such feelings, particularly in the United States. And events are now progressing at a breakneck speed to make a global monarchy a certainty.

Yearly it becomes more difficult for a nation to stand alone. The United States, for example, has felt the impact of lessened Middle East oil imports, more than we would like to admit. Because our economy cannot survive without mobility, oil is as precious as gold. During the height of the gas shortage in Los Angeles in the spring of 1978, I sat in a car for nearly 2 hours waiting to be served. During those hours, I was well aware of the "Siamese" union between the U.S. and Iran—we cannot live together and we cannot live without each other. The man who solves such energy problems will be hailed as greater than Caesar and wiser than Solomon.

The rapid shrinking of the dollar has everyone deeply concerned. There are now places in the United States where the "average new home" sells for $112,000. A generation ago, only the extremely wealthy person could afford such a mortgage. What will the economy be like in another generation? Some economists say the "average home" will sell for between $250,000 and $500,000.

Once this nation was considered the economic mainstay of the world. No longer. Indeed, this economy is a laughingstock in some parts of free Europe. A coming world czar will someday proclaim his ability to stabilize the entire world economy. And when he demonstrates he can back that claim, he will be accepted with open arms.

The Middle East continues to be a boiling pot. I have often visited that part of the world. The tension in the air does not escape the observant visitor. Is the Egypt-Israel peace pact the answer? We can only hope so. But there will come a day when a world leader will declare he has the answer to the conflict. And the whole world, including the Palestinians, will accept his edict.

The world dictator is coming. His reign will be brief. But near the end of that rule, his bloody purges will make the French Revolution look like a

Sunday school picnic. He will be toppled from power by Jesus Christ himself.

In his vision on Patmos, the apostle John saw the rise of this amazing figure:

> And I stood upon the sand of the sea, and saw a beast rise up out of the sea, having seven heads and ten horns, and upon his horns ten crowns, and upon his heads the name of blasphemy. And the beast which I saw was like unto a leopard, and his feet were as the feet of a bear, and his mouth as the mouth of a lion: and the dragon gave him his power, and his seat, and great authority (Revelation 13:1, 2).

Much of the world's history is in Shelley's classic poem "Ozymandius":

> I met a traveller from an antique land
> Who said: "Two vast and trunkless legs of stone
> Stand in the desert. Near them, on the sand,
> Half sunk, a shattered visage lies, whose frown,
> And wrinkled lip, and sneer of cold command,
> Tell that the sculptor well those passions read. . .
> And on the pedestal these words appear—
> 'My name is Ozymandius, king of kings:
> Look on my works, ye Mighty, and despair!'
> Nothing beside remains. Round the decay
> Of that colossal wreck, boundless and bare
> The lone and level sands stretch far away."

So many have tried to fulfill their self-image of world dictator. They have come and gone like the morning mist — the Nebuchadnezzars, Alexanders, the Caesars, the czars, the Lenins, the Hitlers and Napoleons. Some of them did not even leave marked graves. Outside of their futile boasts, nothing remains, and the lone and level sands of their evil lives stretch far away.

It has not been difficult for these self-appointed rulers to make their mark on the world. Mankind has always looked to man himself for ultimate leadership.

In 1979, ancient Persia leaped onto the front pages under the name of Iran. The Shah was deposed. Bahktiar had his moment in the sun. But Khomeini, the voice from afar that rocked Iran, came home triumphantly from exile. Pandemonium welcomed the frail, white-bearded hero of the anti-Shah revolution back to his homeland. The Iranians looked for "the man" who would lead them to their concept of greatness.

Museums around the world stand as mute evidence of the folly of this pursuit. Man is not much closer to peaceful relationships with his fellowmen than he has ever been. But still he seeks for one of his own to reach the ultimate goals of life.

So it will be a natural for Satan when he decides to launch his masterpiece of evil on this planet. The beloved apostle John was banished by Rome to an island of exile 1900 years ago. There, in a mountain cave, he was ushered into the presence of God and given a glimpse of the final dictator who would come into the world.

John's words sound like an unsolvable riddle, but they are not. Man's conflicts are going to climax when Satan fires his last shot at the world—his masterpiece of cruelty and deception—all wrapped up in a person known as the Antichrist. The entire world will embrace his coming and herald him as absolute authority and king.

Antichrist, also known as the beast, will set in

order a system characterized by lawlessness, godlessness, and complete tyranny. Antichrist will have one goal: to exterminate every vestige of Christianity in the world by destroying every person who follows Jesus and outlawing God from his domain. The entire world will worship Satan.

"I saw a beast rise up out of the sea." The sea refers to the sea of nations, which so resembles a troubled ocean. Empires roar and crash like waves. But out of this sea of humanity, an incredible man will come with strange powers and charisma.

Then John wrote, "It had seven heads and ten horns." No earthly creature has 7 heads and 10 horns. But in Revelation 17:12 there is a clear definition of the 10 horns: "And the ten horns which thou sawest are ten kings." So this beast or creature will have the backing of a federation of nations.

Seven colossal empires or "heads" of government are paramount in human history: Egypt, Assyria, Babylon, Medo-Persia, Greece, Rome, and a current amalgamation of nations, particularly those of the Western Hemisphere. This Antichrist will be the sum total of them all in his scope of power and influence. Everything about his demeanor will be blasphemous to a holy God.

John wrote that he would have the appearance of a leopard, bear, and lion. The Old Testament prophet Daniel wrote of these three animals as characteristic of early world powers.

"And the dragon gave him... power." The dragon is Satan himself. In the history of mankind there have been wise and just rulers who served their nations in the fear of God, calling upon divine might and wisdom. But not this ruler, not Antichrist. He will be energized by Satan.

The world will get a firsthand glimpse of Satan's power in the Antichrist. Satan is going to endue him with an incredible, superhuman capacity to succeed. For one thing, he will work miracles. Second Thessalonians 2:9 indicates that Satan will send his beast to do all sorts of signs and wonders and miracles.

Antichrist's biggest trick will be a false solution to the Middle East problems. It will be a political miracle. How the nations will applaud! Israel will believe that he is a friend; that the enormous spending for defense can be stopped finally and the guard relaxed. They will learn too late that it was a trick of the cruelest dimensions. The scene will be set for Armageddon, the final military showdown on the plains around Megiddo.

Not long ago, I stood on that vast plain—the place Napoleon called the greatest natural battlefield in the world—with an Israeli army captain. He had fought in every war for freedom since 1948. He knew the Golan Heights and Negev like the back of his hand. I asked him if he expected another war. Surely peace would come to his land. Surely he could lay down his proverbial sword and shield and have rest.

He looked at me with sad eyes and said, "Oh, there will be one more war, one more war." I tried to brighten the conversation. I said, "You Israelis have such unusual names for your wars such as the War of Yom Kippur and Six Days War. What will you call this next battle?" For a moment I could hear only the blowing of the wind and the distant whine of Phantom jets over Mount Carmel. Then the captain answered in a whisper, "Armageddon."

When a man appears who can offer a solution to the crushing energy problems, to the racial tensions worldwide, to the unrelenting cancer of crime in the streets, to the endless spiral of inflation everywhere, to the heartbreak of Israel and Egypt, to the mass buildup of weapons, and to the starving millions of this world, I guarantee you he will be welcomed with open arms and fanatic devotion. Antichrist's reception on this planet will make the welcome given to other conquerors look like an Irish wake! The world will thunder its applause.

You ask, "When will this beast or Antichrist come?" No one knows. But I know this—the world is getting ready for him. The stage is being set. The players have been given their lines. The overture of chaos has been orchestrated. The houselights are growing dim. The rapture of the Church will be the curtain raiser. It could be at any time.

One of the major signs of the times is Satan's counterfeiting. Satan has never had an original thought in his life. Satan can only imitate. God the Heavenly Father sent Jesus to bring life to this world. Satan will also present a "son" to this planet—the Antichrist. Not to save it or help it, but to destroy it.

Jesus came to give; Antichrist will come to take. Jesus came to build and help. Antichrist will come to devastate. Just as Jesus could only do the will of His Father, so Antichrist can only do that which Satan directs. But I have great news for you! Antichrist will be spectacularly unsuccessful. His term in office will be a short one—just a few years. In that time he will have caused worldwide havoc. God will say, "Enough," and He will send His Son Jesus to stop it.

When Jesus came the first time to this world, He came as a babe at Bethlehem. The second time He comes it will be as a conqueror. John's vision included a glimpse of that historic moment:

> Then I saw heaven opened and a white horse standing there; and the one sitting on the horse [Jesus Christ] was named "Faithful and True." . . . His eyes were like flames, and on his head were many crowns. A name was written on his forehead, and only he knew its meaning. He was clothed with garments dipped in blood, and his title was "The Word of God." The armies of heaven, dressed in finest linen, white and clean, followed him on white horses.
>
> In his mouth he held a sharp sword to strike down the nations; he ruled them with an iron grip; and he trod the winepress of the fierceness of the wrath of Almighty God. On his robe and thigh was written this title: "King of Kings and Lord of Lords."
>
> Then I saw the Evil Creature [Antichrist] gathering the governments of the earth and their armies to fight against the one sitting on the horse and his army. And the Evil Creature was captured, and with him the False Prophet. . . .Both of them . . . were thrown alive into the Lake of Fire that burns with sulphur. And their entire army was killed with the sharp sword in the mouth of the one riding the white horse, and all the birds of heaven were gorged with their flesh (Revelation 19:11-16, 19-21, *The Living Bible*).

So the beast, the Antichrist, becomes only another tyrant. His boasts had echoed through every world capitol, "Look on me, ye mighty, and despair!"

But in eternity I will stand by my King, Jesus Christ, and look for any remains of Antichrist's tyranny. Nothing will remain. *And the lone and level sands of earth's time will have stretched far away.*

# 6
# THE TRIBULATION

No imagination could set forth an accurate portrayal of the Great Tribulation, which is coming upon this planet. Words used in Scripture to describe this 7-year period are *always* negative. You will find such words as judgment, indignation, trial, trouble, destruction, darkness, desolation, and punishment. It only seems logical to this "old retired newsman" that none of these terms seems to fit into God's plan for His church, His Son's bride.

Think, if you will, of a gentleman proposing to the girl of his dreams: "Darling, if you will only consent to marry me, I promise to take you into a time of judgment, indignation, trial, trouble, etc." It doesn't fit. It isn't logical.

However, on the other side of the coin, it seems to me it would be foolish to say God's people in the Western world will never know difficult times. It is possible for our affairs to turn topsy-turvy, and that quite speedily. Governments usually have their best chance of falling in times of economic instability. Many Christians throughout the world have suffered terribly at the hands of their fellowmen. Watchman Nee, for example, died in a concentration camp behind the Bamboo Curtain. But it is one thing to fall into the hands of an angry government; *it is quite another thing to fall into the hands of an angry God!*

The threefold purpose of the Tribulation will be: to purify Israel, to judge sinners, and to punish the Gentile nations for their treatment of God's people and gospel. It will be a time of showing, in its most insidious form, the lawlessness of a satanic regime. None of these things has the remotest tie with the believer. Therefore, by what logic would God cause His people to suffer the intensity of these years?

And yet there seems to be a growing number of Christians who feel the Church will be involved in at least some part of the Tribulation. *I am not among them!* I will list my reasons as we go along. Let's read God's description of these awful years:

> And the kings of the earth, and the great men, and the rich men, and the chief captains, and the mighty men, and every bondman, and every free man, hid themselves in the dens and in the rocks of the mountains; and said to the mountains and rocks, Fall on us, and hide us from the face of him that sitteth on the throne, and from the wrath of the Lamb: for the great day of his wrath is come; and who shall be able to stand? (Revelation 6:15-17).

Is this what Paul promised for believers? "For the *grace* of God that bringeth *salvation* hath appeared to all men, teaching us that, denying ungodliness and worldly lusts, we should live soberly, righteously, and godly, in this present world; *looking for that blessed hope,* and the glorious appearing of the great God and our Saviour Jesus Christ" (Titus 2:11-13). The words *grace, salvation,* and *hope* are not in any way connected to the Tribulation phrases of *wrath, judgment,* and *punishment.*

For those who would equate God's wrath with that of man, I would suggest they recall Pharaoh of Egypt and his experience with supernatural judgment. We living Christians may suffer much of man's judgment before the endtime, but I firmly believe we will not be dealt God's judgment as was Pharaoh. "There is therefore now *no condemnation* to them which are in Christ Jesus" (Romans 8:1).

It also seems that mid-Tribulationists could pinpoint the exact day of Jesus' return if their point of view is correct. Jesus told us no one knows that date: "But of that day and hour knoweth no man, no, not the angels of heaven, but my Father only" (Matthew 24:36). If the Rapture were to take place in mid-Tribulation, any school child who could count could point out the coming of the Lord to the very day.

Paul makes it crystal clear to the church at Thessalonica that the Tribulation would be characterized by the advent of the Antichrist. The Thessalonians were going through difficult times of persecution. Some thought perhaps they were in the dreaded Tribulation. Not so said the apostle.

> We beseech you, brethren, by the coming of our Lord Jesus Christ, and by our gathering together unto him, that ye be not soon shaken in mind, or be troubled, neither by spirit, nor by word, nor by letter as from us, as that the day of Christ is at hand. . . . that day shall not come, except there

> come a falling away first, and *that man of sin be revealed,* the son of perdition (2 Thessalonians 2:1-3).

There is no time that Paul even hints at the Church going through the season of God's visitation of wrath on earth. The judgment of the Church took place at Calvary, and the penalty for our sin was paid at dreadful cost. It need never be paid again.

Another point of logic to be made here is that of the consistency of the Word of God. It never breaks down at any point. At every place in Scripture where God poured out His judgment, *His people were always evacuated first.* Before the flood ravaged the earth, Noah was instructed to build an ark of salvation. Before fire and brimstone devastated the twin cities of Sodom and Gomorrah, Lot and his family were given the chance to flee. While there were times God's people were called upon to endure the wrath of men, never were they made to cringe under God's anger. Will God change his *modus operandi* in the case of the Tribulation? No. It does not stand to reason. God is *immutable*—never changing. His laws will not break down at this point.

Thank God for that truth. No rational believer wants to be left on this earth when God removes all restraint from His anger. The apostle John left no room for conjecture about the terror of that day: "The great day of his wrath is come" (Revelation 6:17). John also refers to the "wine of the wrath of God" and the "winepress of the wrath of God" (14:10, 19). Vials full of the "wrath of God" will be poured out upon the earth (15:7; 16:1), and all nations shall taste of the "cup of the wine of the fierceness of his wrath" (16:19).

Jesus himself testified that this time will be so horrible that "except those days should be shortened [or terminated], there should no flesh be saved" (Matthew 24:22). Revelation 8 and 9 give us some horrifying statistics about the Tribulation:

—A third part of the trees are burnt up.
—A third part of the sea becomes blood.
—A third part of the creatures die.
—A third part of the ships are destroyed.
—A third part of the rivers are hit by fire.
—A third part of the waters are poisoned.
—A third part of the sun is darkened.
—A third part of the stars are darkened.
—A third part of the moon is darkened.
—A third part of the day will be with no sunshine.
—A third part of men will be slain.

The Tribulation will make the European holocaust look like a Sunday afternoon tea party. And all of this death and destruction takes place in a few short months. No wonder Jesus said God would have to terminate His anger before everyone here died. Thank God the Church will be gone.

It is worthy of note that one of the greatest "prayer meetings" in history will take place during this time. All the kings, great and rich men, captains, mighty men, etc., will pray in that day—not for forgiveness (they will be well past that stage)—but for death!

The 7 years of Tribulation will be divided into equal parts of 3½ years.

> And he [Antichrist] shall confirm the covenant [his peace proposals for the world and specifically Israel] with many for one week [prophetically, a seven-year period]: and in the midst of the week he shall cause the sacrifice and the oblation to cease, and for the overspreading of abominations he shall make it desolate, even until the consummation, and that determined shall be poured upon the desolate (Daniel 9:27).

It is halfway through the Tribulation when Antichrist shows his true colors, his satanic origin, and pushes the planet into terror.

Israel, which trusted his peace overtures and began disarmament proceedings, will now find herself ravaged. And Antichrist will inform the world that he is not only the human leader but he is also to be worshiped as divinity. He will cause the worship of himself to originate from the rebuilt temple in Jerusalem ("of abominations he shall make it desolate"). With all manner of signs and wonders by himself and the false prophet, he will persuade the citizens of the world that he is, indeed, the Messiah—*Antichrist* means substitute redeemer or messiah.

His sacrilege of the temple will usher in the second half of the Tribulation, known as the Great Tribulation. It is during this time that God's anger will reach its zenith. The entire visitation of judgment will end at a place called Armageddon.

But the end will not come before a long parade of human woe is strewn across the entire race: the false peace movement which brings the world under one ruler; a worldwide famine, poverty, and want; God's judgment of Russia and her friends (see Ezekiel 38 and 39) and the encroachment of the largest army in human history.

God's dealing with the Soviet bloc warrants attention in our treatment of prophetic events. United States President Jimmy Carter has high hopes for SALT II and has staked a good deal of his own prestige upon it. He said recently: "A SALT treaty will lessen the danger of nuclear destruction, while safeguarding our military security in a more stable, predictable, and peaceful world."

SALT is not a disarmament treaty. It attempts to regulate the strategic balance of military force between the two superpowers. Technically, it does this by allowing each nation a force that could suffer a surprise atomic attack and still be able to launch a devastating counter-attack.

Will the treaty work? Probably not—especially in the light of Ezekiel 38 and 39, where God makes some revelations concerning the rise of the great power to the north of Palestine.

A survey of prophetic Scripture reveals that there will be four major, powerful nations at the time of "the last days." They revolve around Israel, or Palestine. There is the King of the North, the King of the South, the King of the West (the head of the federated states of Europe or Antichrist), and the Kings of the East, an amalgamation of powers beyond the Euphrates River. Ezekiel 38 and 39 deals primarily with the King of the North.

We must remember Ezekiel's prophecies were concerned with the restoration of Israel in the land then known as Palestine. The prophet ministered when the Children of Israel were in Babylonian captivity. They naturally were discouraged. But through Ezekiel they learned that God still had a very important place for them in the future.

They learned there would be a great return to the land, which I believe we are seeing in our lifetime. However, the return did not guarantee spiritual life to the Jews. Indeed, a traveler is hard pressed to see a moving of the Holy Spirit in present-day Israel. What event would take place to bring them to God and to a revelation of His Son Jesus Christ?

Through Ezekiel we learn God is going to do a fantastic thing in Israel that will convince them He is on the throne and in total control. They will be shaken as few people in history.

"The word of the Lord came unto me, saying, Son of man, set thy face against Gog, the land of Magog, the chief prince of Meshech and Tubal, and prophesy against him" (Ezekiel 38:1, 2).

What are these strange names? Do they have any relevance to us today? I believe they do. Genesis 10 lists the descendants of Noah's sons, Shem, Ham, and Japheth. It is Japheth's family that concerns us. In verse 2 we are told of his sons, Gomer, Magog, Madai, Javan, Tubal, and Meshech. So the names correspond to those in Ezekiel 38. What is important about these sons of Japheth? There is good reason to believe that, following the Flood, these people migrated from Turkey (the site of Mt. Ararat) to the north, past the Caspian Sea and the Black Sea—into the area we know today as Soviet Russia.

At this point in Ezekiel's prophecy, this northern power has moved against the land of Israel and is winning. God has to intervene to save the Jews.

> And I will turn thee back, and put hooks into thy jaws, and I will bring thee forth, and all thine army, horses and horsemen, all of them clothed with all sorts of armor, even a great company with bucklers and shields, all of them handling swords (Ezekiel 38:4).

Verse 6 indicates that Russia will have allies in the fight against Israel. The plot takes a fascinating turn in verses 10-12:

> Thus saith the Lord God; It shall also come to pass, that at the same time shall things come into thy mind, and thou shalt think an evil thought: and thou shalt say, I will go up to the land of unwalled villages; I will go to them that are at rest, that dwell safely, all of them dwelling without walls, and having neither bars nor gates, to take a spoil, and to take a prey.

This certainly doesn't describe current-day Israel. She is not a country of unwalled villages, nor is she at rest. "Having neither bars nor gates" is a joke to anyone who has traveled extensively in the Middle East.

I have stood on the ruins of Megiddo and looked west toward the slopes of Mount Carmel and watched those fantastic Phantom jets, piloted by crack Israeli warriors, pierce the sky.

On the 25th anniversary of Israel's nationhood, I was near the Wailing Wall when a squadron of the Phantoms swooped in over the Mount of Olives, hitting their afterburners over the Kidron Valley and causing a cacophony of sound such as I have never heard. By the time they crossed the Temple Mount, they were only a few hundred feet in the air. Suddenly, the pilots stood those jets on their tails and pushed them straight into the sky, leaving behind multicolor vapors. It was spectacular! The thousands of gathered Israelis screamed their delight.

I have watched Israeli tanks on maneuvers. All over that ancient land I have seen the male and female soldiers, their Uzi's (automatic rifles) slung over their shoulders, ever watchful. I have seen the machine gun holes in the national airport, the result of terrorist attacks. A place of unwalled villages? A nation at rest? Not now! Not on your life.

Then what will cause that nation to make an about-face during the Tribulation and enter into disarmament? The Israeli leadership, so tired of constant war and the expenditure of the greatest part of Israel's funds for armament, will believe Antichrist's boast that he is the great peacemaker. And for a time, he will live up to his promise. There will finally be peace in the land.

But suddenly—midway through the Tribulation — there is an attack! Russia and her allies swoop down on the little nation like vultures on a rabbit. Israel is defenseless. She hasn't a chance.

But notice Ezekiel 38:18, 19:

> And it shall come to pass at the same time when Gog shall come against the land of Israel, saith the Lord God, that my fury shall come up in my face. For in my jealousy and in the fire of my wrath have I spoken, Surely in that day there shall be a great shaking in the land of Israel.

God sees the Russian forces sweep into Israel. But God is in command! He will use the attackers as the greatest object lesson of all time. God moves swiftly:

> I will call for a sword against him [Russia] throughout all my mountains, said the Lord God: every man's sword shall be against his brother. And I will plead against him with pestilence and with blood; and I will rain upon him, and upon his bands, and upon the many people that are with him, an overflowing rain, and great hailstones, fire, and brimstone. Thus I will magnify myself, and sanctify myself; and I will be known in the eyes of many nations, and they shall know that I am the Lord (Ezekiel 38:21-23).

Why does God intervene? To honor the protests of other nations? No! Not even to give validity to Israel itself. He intervenes to bring honor to His own name. Read about the devastation God inflicts on the attackers in Ezekiel 39:

> Son of man, prophesy against Gog, and say, Thus saith the Lord God; behold I am against thee, O Gog, the chief prince of Meshech and Tubal: and I will turn thee back, and leave but the sixth part of thee, and I will cause thee to come up from the north parts, and will bring thee upon the mountains of Israel: and I will smite thy bow out of thy left hand, and will cause thine arrows to fall out of thy right hand. Thou shalt fall upon the mountains of Israel, thou, and all thy bands, and the people that is with thee: I will give thee unto the ravenous birds of every sort, and to the beasts of the field, to be devoured. . . . And I will send a fire on Magog, and among them that dwell carelessly in the isles: and they shall know that I am the Lord (vv. 1-4, 6).

God's intentions are made clear in verse 7: "So

will I make my holy name known in the midst of my people Israel; and I will not let them pollute my holy name any more: and the heathen shall know that I am the Lord, the Holy One in Israel." What a revival there will be! It will be the giving of life to the dry bones of Ezekiel 37.

Ezekiel's prophetic writing tells us the death rate will be so high it will take 7 months just to bury the fallen. The stench will be so unbearable that travelers journeying in Israel will have to stop their noses because of the corruption.

Will Israel have peace and rest now? No. For with Russia and her allies out of the way, Antichrist and his coalition of western nations will now attempt to consolidate power in the Holy City. Satan's beast will be in temporary control. He will have power "over all kindreds, and tongues, and nations. And all that dwell upon the earth shall worship him" (Revelation 13: 7, 8).

But not for long.

Armageddon will be just around the corner. And the human blood has only begun to flow.

# 7
# ARMAGEDDON

The little city of Nazareth lies tucked in the dusty hills that overlook a vast plain to the immediate south. I have often wondered if Jesus ever wandered out on one of those picturesque bluffs just as the sun was slipping behind Mount Carmel to look down on that great plain. The Prince of Peace surveying the site of the greatest battle in human history, a battle in which He will play the key role. What a dramatic setting!

The plain just below Nazareth is Jezreel or Armageddon. Napoleon Bonaparte once marched across it and called it "the greatest natural battlefield on earth." The Tribulation will be brought to an end there, when Christ returns to earth to triumph over the largest amalgamation of troops ever assembled.

What events will lead to this struggle? Once again, Satan will be the prime mover, seeking to destroy every living Jew to circumvent God's plan of the ages. Satan will use his "counterfeit christ" to fulfill his plan.

Once in power, Antichrist will do anything Satan desires. And following God's crushing of the Soviet bloc, his every move will be intrinsically evil.

> And the king [that is, Antichrist] shall do according to his will; and he shall exalt himself, and magnify himself above every god, and shall speak marvelous things against the God of gods, and shall prosper till the indignation be accomplished: for that that is determined shall be done. Neither shall he regard the God of his fathers, nor the desire of women, nor regard any god: for he shall magnify himself above all (Daniel 11:36, 37).

No one knows God's Word better than Satan. He knows the Jews are God's chosen ones and God has always used that nation to bring about His earthly plans. It is only logical to assume that, if the Jews can be annihilated, God's plans can then be circumvented and Satan's regime made safe.

I have read every book on the life of Adolph Hitler that I can find. As I have pored over the details of his career, I have become convinced *the Fuhrer* was totally demon-possessed. The more power he gained, the more maniacal his hatred of the Jews became. Satan used Hitler to try to bypass God's plan of the ages. I have worn out two copies of Shirer's *Rise and Fall of the Third Reich* in cataloging the many times between 1935 and 1945 God supernaturally intervened to stop Hitler and the Nazis. There can be little doubt about God's hand in the Fuhrer's destruction: from the premature winter storm in Russia, just as the German soldiers had the Kremlin in their sight, to the weird dreams and visitations Hitler experienced when he could have been destroying allied troops at Dunkirk.

I have walked through the ruins of those European concentration camps, where the human horrors defied all possible description. There is still a tangible feeling of evil that pervades those places. Satan was destroyed in his efforts in the early 1940s, but he will try again to form a "final solution" to God's people. But this time, the attempt will end—not with atomic bombs and D-days—with an incredible invasion led by Jesus himself!

The persecution of the Jews will begin midway through the Tribulation period. Antichrist will remove his mask of friendship and toss away his proposals for Mideast peace.

> And when the dragon [Satan] saw that he was cast unto the earth, he persecuted the woman [Israel] which brought forth the man child [Jesus]. And to the woman were given two wings of a great eagle, that she might fly into the wilderness, into her place, where she is nourished for a time, and times, and half a time [3½ years] from the face of the serpent (Revelation 12:13, 14).

It will be open war between Satan and the chosen people of God. But there is a fascinating verse in Daniel that introduces a facet of the battle that is strictly supernatural:

> He [Antichrist] shall enter also into the glorious land [Israel], and many countries shall be overthrown: but these shall escape out of his hand, even Edom, and Moab, and the chief of the children of Ammon (Daniel 11:41).

Apparently the only place outside of the Asiatic

nations where Antichrist cannot gain power is the present-day country of Jordan. There is no rational reason for such a thing, outside of the divine will of God.

When the persecution begins in full fury, following Antichrist's abominating the holy temple in Jerusalem, the Jews will have one escape hatch—across the Jordan River to the land currently ruled by King Hussein. Many scholars are giving more and more credence to the lost city of Petra, built by Esau thousands of years ago, as a harbor for the Jews during the Tribulation period.

Jesus told of this flight into the wilderness:

> When ye therefore shall see the abomination of desolation, spoken of by Daniel the prophet [see Daniel 9:27], stand in the holy place [Antichrist's desecration of the temple in Jerusalem], . . . then let them which be in Judea flee into the mountains [current-day Jordan]: let him which is on the housetop not come down to take anything out of his house: neither let him which is in the field return back to take his clothes. And woe unto them that are with child, and to them which give suck in those days [it will be so difficult for mothers with nursing children to flee the country]! But pray ye that your flight be not in winter [I have been marooned in Jerusalem by a snowstorm!], neither on the sabbath day [for a Jew will not travel very far on that day because of the Mosaic law]: for then shall be great tribulation, such as was not since the beginning of the world to this time, no, nor ever shall be (Matthew 24:15-21).

Jesus made it plain that Antichrist's terror would be at its peak during this time. Apparently nothing will stand in Satan's way. Perhaps the Jews will be destroyed this time.

Suddenly, "Tidings out of the east and out of the north shall trouble him [Antichrist]" (Daniel 11:44). Someone brings Antichrist some very bad news. There is a threat to his power. John saw the attackers in his divine vision:

> And the sixth angel sounded, and I heard a voice from the four horns of the golden altar which is before God, saying to the sixth angel which had the trumpet, Loose the four angels which are bound in the great river Euphrates. And the four angels were loosed, which were prepared for an hour, and a day, and a month, and a year, for to slay the third part of men. And the number of the army of the horsemen were two hundred thousand thousand. . . . And the sixth angel poured out his vial upon the great river Euphrates; and the water thereof was dried up, that the way of the kings of the east might be prepared (Revelation 9:13-16; 16:12).

Here comes an alliance of nations (Asiatic, in my opinion) to confront Antichrist and his western nations. It is an army of 200 million troops en route to wipe out Antichrist. Little wonder the news troubles him! It not only troubles him, it also infuriates him so much that Daniel said: "He shall go forth with great fury to destroy, and utterly to make away many. And he shall plant the tabernacles of his palace between the seas in the glorious holy mountain" (Daniel 11:44, 45). The seas are the Mediterranean and the Dead Sea and the place Antichrist decides to make his stand is Jerusalem, the holy city.

What a dramatic setting. Try to imagine it if you

can. Jerusalem and all Judea, the length and breadth of Israel, are an armed camp, staffed by Satan, Antichrist, and their legions. They are preparing for an attack from the east by 200 million troops. The fight is about to start.

But suddenly, a third army attacks! It is an army the other two combatants did not know existed:

> And I saw heaven opened, and behold a white horse; and he that sat upon him was called Faithful and True, and in righteousness he doth judge and make war. His eyes were as a flame of fire, and on his head were many crowns; and he had a name written, that no man knew, but he himself. And he was clothed with a vesture dipped in blood: and his name is called The Word of God. And the armies which were in heaven followed him upon white horses, clothed in fine linen, white and clean. And out of his mouth goeth a sharp sword, that with it he should smite the nations; and he shall rule them with a rod of iron (Revelation 19:11-15).

What a shocking development! Two armies, poised for battle, suddenly look up and see a third army rapidly descending from the sky. The airborne invaders are led by a Figure who strikes terror in their hearts. They quickly forget their common hatred of each other and make arrangements to meet the third invader: "I saw the beast [Antichrist], and the kings of the earth, and their armies, gathered together to make war against him that sat on the horse, and against his army" (Revelation 19:19).

Earth's armies will then hear a noise unlike

anything they have ever heard, louder than a million jet planes, more damaging than any weapon. The Psalmist was given a vision of this incredible moment:

> Why do the heathen rage, and the people imagine a vain thing? The kings of the earth set themselves, and the rulers take counsel together, against the Lord, and against his Anointed, saying, Let us break their bands asunder, and cast away their cords from us.
>
> He that sitteth in the heavens shall laugh: the Lord shall have them in derision. Then shall he speak unto them in his wrath, and vex them in his sore displeasure. *Yet have I set my King upon my holy hill of Zion* (Psalm 2:1-6).

The derisive laughter of God will fill the sky, shaking cities. Men will fall to the ground, quaking with terror. That laughter—what an awful sound!—tearing at the very souls of men. So Antichrist was a lie! It was all a hoax. He was not God after all. What a chilling revelation that will be!

Imagine the fighter planes taking off from various air bases in the Mideast. Their target is the One on the lead horse. Heat-seeking missiles are directed at Him and His followers. Multiplied millions of rifles are aimed at His heart. As He draws ever closer to the Mount of Olives, earth's troops mass around the foot of the slopes to cut Him off. The terrible laughter from the skies is driving them crazy. Then—the laughter stops and a thundering voice is heard; it is directed to the One on the white horse: "Thou shalt break them with a rod of iron; thou shalt dash them in pieces like a potter's vessel" (Psalm 2:9). The Rider on the white horse opens His mouth to give a divine directive, and the end of the earthly coalition comes quickly.

Now the world is confronted with Jesus Christ again. The last time they met, Jesus was nailed to a cross and executed. But this time they see a different aspect of His personality. He is no longer a lamb, but a mighty monarch. He has returned to rule the earth. "For as the Father hath life in himself; so hath he given to the Son to have life in himself; and hath given him authority to execute judgment also, because he is the Son of man" (John 5:26, 27).

What weapon destroys the earth's armies? A magnificent one. Christ descends to this planet, where His feet will touch again the top of Mount Olivet. All the redeemed saints who were raptured 7 years previously, who have been audited at the judgment seat of Christ and who have thrilled to the presence of Christ at the Marriage Supper, return with Him. They are coming to implement the 1,000-year reign. But first there is the matter of Antichrist and his army, as well as the 200 million troops of the Asiatic coalition. What destroys them? Do the saints have to fight their first moment back on earth? No.

John saw a sharp sword proceeding out of the mouth of Christ. With a simple spoken word, He will end all human hostility to His lordship. In the beginning, God *spoke*—and all creation came into being. At the end, it will be the same—God *speaks*. The power of the spoken word, proceeding from Jesus' lips, will end the resistance at Armageddon.

> I saw an angel standing in the sun; and he cried with a loud voice, saying to all the fowls that fly in

> the midst of heaven, Come and gather yourselves together unto the supper of the great God; that ye may eat the flesh of kings, and the flesh of captains, and the flesh of mighty men, and the flesh of horses, and of them that sit on them, and the flesh of all men, both free and bond, both small and great (Revelation 19:17, 18).

It's over. Imagine the incredible scene. Bodies are strewn over the landscape. Every weapon of war has been destroyed in a split second. The fighter planes have fallen from the sky without being touched. There is a haze everywhere. And silence. Terrible, gripping silence. Only a slight blowing of the wind can be heard.

> The beast was taken, and with him the false prophet that wrought miracles before him, with which he deceived them that had received the mark of the beast, and them that worshipped his image. These both were cast alive into a lake of fire burning with brimstone (Revelation 19:20).

Christ will set up His millennial reign, with His throne located in Jerusalem. There will be a theocratic administration—God-rule—on this planet. Congresses will be no more; neither will there be parliaments. No more elections. No senates. Jesus' Word will be the final law. Pain and sickness will be banished. There can be no death in His divine presence. Satan will have long since been bound for the 1,000 years of the millennial kingdom. And Jesus will reign from sea to shining sea. Hallelujah!

# 8

# THE JUDGMENT OF SINNERS

> And I saw a great white throne, and him that sat on it, from whose face the earth and the heaven fled away; and there was found no place for them. And I saw the dead, small and great, stand before God; and the books were opened: and another book was opened, which is the book of life: and the dead were judged out of those things which were written in the books, according to their works.
>
> And the sea gave up the dead which were in it; and death and hell delivered up the dead which were in them: and they were judged every man according to their works. And death and hell were cast into the lake of fire. This is the second death. And whosoever was not found written in the book of life was cast into the lake of fire (Revelation 20:11-15).

In my news career, I covered many trials. Many were murder trials. Others were robbery. The saddest trial I ever saw was that of a young man accused of armed robbery.

I suppose the trial took on added dimensions to me because the accused was a friend of mine. We had gone to school together, marched in ROTC together, played ball together in high school. My friend Jack (not his real name) was a moody kid and was usually in and out of trouble. I thought he had a good future ahead of him in boxing. He was a lightning-fast middleweight with good hands. But he never stayed in good enough shape to take the punches.

I lost track of him for a while; and then I heard his name on the police radio. Apparently motivated by boredom, he had found a friend's .38 pistol and held up a liquor store.

The burly old proprietor feigned great fear and handed Jack the money he demanded. Being a beginner at robbery, Jack took the money and turned his back to leave the store. As soon as he turned his back, the liquor store owner reached under the counter for a huge pistol, aimed it at Jack's legs, and pulled the trigger. He nearly blew one of my friend's legs off. His apprehension by police was simple, and the trial date was set.

I was shocked when his attorney suggested Jack plead innocent. No one in attendance had any doubt that he was guilty. The evidence was overwhelming. But Jack steadfastly clung to his "not guilty" plea. Finally, the arguments were heard and the jury filed into the deliberation room. And then I saw a stark drama!

Jack suddenly bolted from the defense table and ran to the judge's bench. He fell on his knees and began pleading for mercy, saying over and over again that he was guilty. He begged for mercy. He asked the judge to remember it was his first offense.

The judge looked at him softly. I thought he was going to weep. He said: "Jack, under the rules of jurisprudence in this state, once the jury leaves the dock and goes into deliberation, the plea cannot be changed. If you had come to me 5 minutes ago, asking for mercy, admitting your guilt, I would have taken into consideration everything in your favor. In all probability, I would have given you a suspended sentence. You could be on your way home with your folks right now. But for some strange reason, you insisted you were innocent, and now the jury has gone to deliberate. If they find you guilty, I have no choice but to sentence you to prison."

It was not long before the jury returned to the courtroom and the verdict was offered. "Guilty."

I watched my friend stand before the judge to hear sentence pronounced: "Five years in the state penitentiary."

As they led him out the door to a waiting car, I couldn't help thinking how foolish Jack had been. He should have been on his way home with his parents. Instead he sat manacled between two big guards on his way to the state prison. He had simply waited to change his plea until it was too late.

That scene may be repeated millions of times at the Great White Throne Judgment. After Jesus Christ reigns on this earth for 1,000 years, Satan will be loosed again for a very short season. You see, there will be millions of humans born during the Millennium. They will be given no choice during the Millennium—they will obey the edicts of Christ, who sits on the throne of the world. He is in absolute control.

But God will never violate anyone's will. He knows there will be those, strange as it may seem, who will not wish to continue under Christ's benevolent leadership. They will long for a time in which they can do as they choose, thumbing their noses in God's face. So they will be given the opportunity.

Satan will be loosed and will attract many followers, rejecters of Christ. They will attack the holy city of Jerusalem. Again God will act sovereignly and they will be defeated. And God will bid farewell to this planet, destroying it without a trace, to be replaced by an all-new world.

At this point in the prophetic time scale, the Great White Throne Judgment will take place. What an awesome sight it will be. In his vision, John saw the scene.

Men and women who reject God in their lifetime on earth will be faced with a confrontation with Him. They will cover their faces and try to hide, but there will be no hiding places available. They will give account to God for their sinful lives and their rejection of Jesus Christ as Saviour. At this point God will remove the last traces of sin's curse on mankind. There were three: a curse on the devil, one on the earth, and a curse on sinners.

The latter of those curses was removed at a dreadful cost on Calvary when Jesus bore the curse of sin for fallen man. Paul could write accurately: "There is therefore now no condemnation to them which are in Christ Jesus" (Romans 8:1).

But what about the other two curses? We read of the fall of man in Genesis. It was at that point that God made Satan's future very clear:

> The Lord God said unto the serpent, Because thou hast done this, thou art cursed above all cattle, and above every beast of the field; upon thy

> belly shalt thou go, and dust shalt thou eat all the days of thy life (Genesis 3:14).

What about the other curse? You will find it three verses later:

> And unto Adam he said, Because thou hast hearkened unto the voice of thy wife, and hast eaten of the tree, of which I commanded thee, saying, Thou shalt not eat of it: cursed is the ground for thy sake; in sorrow shalt thou eat of it all the days of thy life; thorns also and thistles shall it bring forth to thee; and thou shalt eat the herb of the field (vv. 17, 18).

Apparently, from John's account of the Great White Throne Judgment in Revelation 20, the earth will vanish. So God will also deal with the earth's curse—by simply destroying every molecule of it. Peter foretold this harsh act: "The heavens shall pass away with a great noise, and the elements shall melt with fervent heat, the earth also and the works that are therein shall be burned up" (2 Peter 3:10).

The earth that served as a stage for man's rebellion against God will no longer be allowed to exist. Think of it—even the elements will be destroyed. We were taught in school that elements cannot be destroyed, only changed molecularly. God says that is not enough. He will dissolve even the elements.

Now we come to the final curse—the one on Satan, and, by affiliation, those who chose to side with him. The wicked dead will be resurrected to meet God. There is no grave, not even a towering monument, able to withstand this divine call to judgment. Monarch or merchant—it will not matter. All that has priority on this awful day are "the books."

There will be two sets of books. God has been the most conscientious bookkeeper in history. One set of books will give the detailed account of every life—every rejection of Christ, every adulterous moment, every filthy word, every vestige of hatred, every word of gossip, every lie, every idolatry, every theft, every sin that God said would destroy mankind. Not a single act, word, or thought will escape that incredible bookkeeping system.

But God keeps another book—the Book of Life. It's a cross-reference. Only those whose names are entered in that sacred book will have eternal life. And the only thing that can blot out the record in the books of works is the blood of Jesus Christ.

Recently, Americans have again sided pro or con on the capital punishment issue. In Florida, a man went to his death in the electric chair. Newspapers and magazines printed the gory details of his death. Many years ago, I was given the "opportunity" as a newsman to be an official witness at an electrocution. I turned it down. That's beyond my call of duty. But as a born-again believer, I will stand somewhere behind the throne of God at the judgment, when sentence is pronounced on the lost. What a horrible moment it will be!

The books will not lie. They are irrefutable. And, "The soul that sinneth, it shall die" (Ezekiel 18:4). The sin that damns all men is a common one—rejection of the Lord Jesus Christ, the absolute, only avenue to eternal life. Jesus said of himself, "I am the way, the truth, and the life: no man cometh unto the Father, but by me" (John 14:6). He couldn't have made it any plainer than that.

Now comes the sentencing: Satan and his entire dominion (the lost, who sided with him against Christ in this life) will be cast into the lake of fire. Eternal punishment, unending, and horrible beyond all description—eternal separation from God.

HELL! The prison house of despair.
Here are some things that won't be there:
No flowers will bloom on the banks of hell,
No beauties of nature we love so well;
No comforts of home, music and song,
No friendship of joy will be found in that throng;
No children to brighten the long, weary night;
No love nor peace nor one ray of light;
No blood-washed soul with face beaming bright,
No loving smile in the region of night;
No mercy, no pity, nor pardon nor grace,
No water, Oh, God, what a terrible place!
The pangs of the lost no human can tell,
Not one moment's ease—there is no rest in hell!

HELL! The prison house of despair.
Here are some things that will be there:
Fire and brimstone will be there, we know,
For God in His Word has told us so;
Memory, remorse, suffering and pain,
Weeping and wailing, but all in vain;
Blasphemers, swearers, haters of God,
Christ-rejecters while here on earth trod;
Murderers, gamblers, drunkards and liars,
Will have their part in the lake of fire;
The filthy, the vile, the cruel and mean,
What a horrible mob in hell will be seen!
Yes, more than humans on earth can tell,
Are the torments and woes of eternal HELL!

Catherine Dangell

The terrible tragedy of their lost state is that it needn't have been. There were ample warnings: loving inquiries, intercessory prayers, church services, radio and television programs, and books such as this one—all pointing sinners to Christ. Like my friend Jack, however, those who will be at the last judgment will have waited too long to change their plea. It will be too late to cast themselves on the mercy of the great Judge.

# 9

# WHAT WILL IT BE LIKE IN HEAVEN?

"In my Father's house are many mansions: if it were not so, I would have told you. I go to prepare a place for you" (John 14:2).

I am always thrilled when I hear someone sing the song, "The Holy City"—especially when they sing the last portion:

*And once again the scene was changed,*
*New earth there seemed to be,*
*I saw the Holy City beside the tideless sea;*
*The light of God was on its streets,*
*The gates were open wide,*
*And all who would might enter,*
*And no one was denied.*
*No need of moon or stars by night*
*Or sun to shine by day;*
*It was the new Jerusalem*
*That would not pass away;*
*It was the new Jerusalem*
*That would not pass away.*
*Jerusalem, Jerusalem!*
*Sing for the night is o'er!*
*Hosanna in the highest,*
*Hosanna forevermore.*

Oh, I wish the Bible told us more about our eternal home. It gives us just the briefest of glimpses of that magnificent city. But this thoroughly tests our spiritual motivation. Why do we serve Jesus? Why do we walk with the redeemed? Is our goal a mansion on some celestial cliff? Are we only after crowns?

Suppose, sir, you had just asked a lovely girl to marry you. And she said to you: "Well, I must think this over. First, tell me about the house you're going to give me. I want a description of every room. Will there be several limousines in the garage? Is the furniture the most expensive you can buy? Are all the chandeliers made of crystal? Now be careful in your description, dear, because my answer to your proposal depends on this house."

You would not have to be too perceptive to realize you had just proposed to a gold digger. She was not nearly as concerned about you as she was about the house.

Our motivation in serving Christ is not just to get to heaven. Oh, that will be wonderful. Every Christian waits expectantly for that trumpet to sound; the signal that we will be taken by Christ to glory. But heaven is a secondary reason for loving Jesus. If there were no heaven, no mansions, no crowns, no eternity with Him, I would still want to be a Christian. Christ is the center of my life. He takes a life that is torn to pieces and makes something very beautiful of it.

Jesus himself is sufficient reason to be a Christian. No other motivation is necessary. But in His great plan of redemption, He has included a place for us in His Father's house, where there are many mansions. Is it any wonder the songwriter penned, “It pays to serve Jesus; it pays every day”?

Although the Bible doesn’t give us a thorough description of heaven, it does tell us enough to know it will be magnificent; transcending anything mortal eyes have beheld.

The apostle John was given a brief vision of the celestial city while he was a prisoner on Patmos. The Book of Revelation gives us the details of the vision. In chapter 21 John wrote: “And God shall wipe away all tears from their eyes; and there shall be no more death, neither sorrow, nor crying, neither shall there be any more pain: for the former things are passed away” (v. 4).

No tears! All of the grief that causes tears will n longer exist. The hurts, the partings, the sorrow that sometimes engulfs this planet, will all have been removed. There will be no tears because there will be nothing to make you cry in heaven.

No death! No more lines of the bereaved standing beside open caskets. No more funeral processions slowly driving to waiting cemeteries. Christian undertakers will have to learn a different profession in heaven; there will be no need of their services there. Death is such a waste, it is a part of the horrible curse of sin. With the exception of Elijah and Enoch, death has visited every man, woman, and child in history. But the Grim Reaper will not be allowed in the Holy City. He will have long since been banished into eternal oblivion, never to curse the human race again. Oh, heaven is going to be a marvelous place. It makes all our trying moments on this earth so worthwhile.

No more sorrow! No more pain! Nothing will be allowed in heaven to mar your life. All who corrupt will have been dealt with summarily. They, too, will have their place, but it will be far removed from heaven:

> But the fearful, and unbelieving, and the abominable, and murderers, and whoremongers, and sorcerers, and idolaters, and all liars, shall have their part in the lake which burneth with fire and brimstone: which is the second death (Revelation 21:8).

Heaven is going to be quite a place. In fact, Jesus said, "I go to prepare a place for you." I'm glad Jesus phrased it like that. Everyone of us needs to feel he has a place. No matter what you do in life or where you may live, it's a terrible sensation to feel you are out of place—you don't belong. Have you ever walked into a room crowded with people and suddenly felt out of place? It isn't pleasant, is it? But that won't happen in heaven. Jesus said you will have a place. It means that in heaven you will be needed, you will be wanted, you will be enjoyed by others, they will want your company. You will always feel at home there.

And heaven will not be just a place; it will be a perfect place. Whatever God creates is perfect. It was Satan who disrupted the whole scheme of life. And Satan will not be around to do it again. He will be banished to the place reserved for him and all the fallen angels. He will never bother a man or woman again. So heaven will be perfect. Every day will be unmarred and untainted.

And it will be permanent. Paul once testified that on this earth he had no continuing city. He meant that he constantly had to travel to other places in his ministry. But even if he could have stayed put, there is no such thing as a permanent city. I have walked through some of the oldest continuously inhabited cities of the world. Although they are thousands of years old, they represent only a grain of sand on the beach of time. They crumble and fall, and even when they are repaired, they crumble again. But heaven will be permanent. A perfect, permanent place!

Have you ever seen cartoons of people floating on clouds, strumming golden harps? That scene is sometimes used to depict heaven. But that would get very boring after a while. Heaven will be far more than just a cloud and a harp. We are going to be extremely busy in heaven. Our activities will be wide and varied. They will keep us occupied throughout all eternity.

John saw the Christians gathered around the heavenly throne, praising God. Their voices sounded like a Niagara of sound (see Revelation 19:1-7). Worship will be one of our primary ministries in the Holy City. It's one of the reasons why we love to praise God right here and now. Not only does it please God, it also serves as a rehearsal for that time when we will gather with every saint who ever lived to lift our voices in worship to God. The Bible says God inhabits the praises of His people.

There will be such singing in heaven! Do you realize the Book of Revelation contains more songs than any other Book of the Bible with the exception of the Psalms? There are 14 grand songs in Revelation. Some of them are sung by the angels. But most of them are sung by the saints, those of us who have been gathered home.

The lyrics are magnificent:

> Salvation to our God which sitteth upon the throne, and unto the Lamb (Revelation 7:10).
>
> Great and marvelous are thy works, Lord God Almighty; just and true are thy ways, thou King of saints. Who shall not fear thee, O Lord, and glorify thy name? For thou only art holy; for all nations shall come and worship before thee; for thy judgments are made manifest (Revelation 15:3, 4).

Can you imagine millions and millions of people all singing together, their voices blended in intricate harmonies—accompanied by an orchestra of thousands times 10 thousands—with the strings, brass, woodwinds, and percussion? It will be more thrilling than all the concerts of earth put together. And, if you know Jesus Christ as your personal Saviour, you will be a part of it!

We are going to have other ministries there. We will serve the Lord; doing His will and bidding throughout the universe. Jesus promised us that if we are faithful in the few things He has given us here, then we will be given vital areas of responsibility there.

We will have delegated authority. Revelation 20 specifically points out that we shall reign over the earth—the new one God has created just for the redeemed.

We will have unlimited potential there. And the fellowship will be fabulous. We will continue to learn. Paul wrote that we see through a glass darkly on this planet. But in heaven we shall continue to learn and grow. And there will be eternal rest; which simply means there will be nothing in heaven to sap our strength, drain our energies, or diffuse our minds.

The songwriter said, "Only glory by and by!" I do not pretend to begin to understand it all. I only know heaven will be a place of infinite blessedness, beyond all human understanding or comprehension. I would not miss it for anything!